Employment ? Personality Tests Decoded

Includes Sample and Practice
Tests for Self-Assessment

By

Anne Hart
with George Sheldon

CAREER
PRESS

Franklin Lakes, NJ

EMPLOYMENT PERSONALITY TESTS DECODED
EDITED BY JODI BRANDON
TYPESET BY EILEEN DOW MUNSON
Cover design by Rob Johnson / Johnson Design
Printed in the U.S.A. by Book-mart Press

To order this title, please call toll-free 1-800-CAREER-1 (NJ and Canada: 201-848-0310) to order using VISA or MasterCard, or for further information on books from Career Press.

The Career Press, Inc., 3 Tice Road, PO Box 687,
Franklin Lakes, NJ 07417
www.careerpress.com

Library of Congress Cataloging-in-Publication Data

Hart, Anne, 1941-
    Crack employment personality tests : includes sample and practice tests for self-assessment / by Anne Hart, with George Sheldon
        p. cm.
    Includes bibliographical references and index.
    ISBN-13: 978-156414-946-6
    ISBN-10: 1-56414-946-3
        1. Employment tests. 2. Ability—Testing. 3. Personality tests. I. Sheldon, George. II. Title.

HF5549.5.E5H37 2007
650.14—dc22

                                                                2006038159

?

To all readers curious
about
personality assessments.

?

? ? ? ? ? ? ? ?

Contents

? ? ? ? ? ? ? ?

Preface

Personality tests encourage self-scrutiny. Simplicity works well when designing personality tests because when people discuss other people's personalities, they describe personality traits in simple, everyday language that's published in dictionaries. Test design is all about foresight, insight, and hindsight into specific words for identity.

The goal of designing any practice personality assessment or test is to help you avoid the pitfalls of an actual test you need to take. By learning about the styles, words, and goals of the tests, you are better prepared for the actual tests. Assessments are created by people that use key words describing personality traits. Those key words end up in dictionaries, and you need to recognize and know them.

I designed my personality tests by looking through the dictionaries and thesauri to find as many words as I could describing the nouns, adverbs, action verbs, and adjectives for character, personality, attitude, and mood.

Then I narrowed down the descriptive, behavioral "tag words" and tag lines to 10 opposite concepts: *grounded vs. verve, rational vs. enthusiastic, traditional vs. change-oriented, decisive vs. investigative, lone vs. outgoing.*It also helped looking through my collected Website list of 1,008 action verbs (*http://annehart.tripod.com/id30.html*). These words also are used on resumes. (See my book on action verbs for communicators, *801 Action Verbs for Communicators: Position Yourself First with Action Verbs for Journalists, Speakers, Educators, Students, Resume-Writers, Editors.*)

The behavior or actions lead to definitions of character and personality. The roots of all of these meanings are found in dictionaries and thesauri, as had been researched in the past by scientists seeking definitions in lexicons of personality traits.

For example, Arabs call an angry person *dib* or *bear*. A clever man evading the corrupted aspects of the law is called a *deeb* or *wolf*.

There are coffee klatch words in many languages used as shorthand to define personality traits or aspects. In Hebrew, a *schlimazel* is an aggressive leader. A *schlemiel* is a receptive follower (who usually gets victimized by the *schlimazel*). In Yiddish a *maven* is an expert with experience.

Those vernacular words from around the world end up in dictionaries and thesauri, often translated into English-language dictionaries, and most often focusing on a variety of personality aspects. These definitions help me design tests.

Often, it is the linguists and novelists who contribute the roots or foundation to personality assessment design and tests of abstract thinking, cognitive intelligence, and reading comprehension assessments. When I design personality tests, I don't go to the established tests based on the studies of previous psychoanalysts. Instead, I go to the bare bones, the roots of how personality is defined—and the roots of the definitions of character, personality, attitude, and emotional maturity are all defined in the most basic dictionaries and thesaurus.

Those who study behavioral sciences are familiar with the "lexical hypothesis." A good description of the lexical hypothesis appears in Anne Murphy Paul's book, *The Cult of Personality*. (She exposes the flawed theories and faulty methods that render their results unreliable and invalid. Personality tests, she contends, produce descriptions of people that are nothing like human beings as they actually are: complicated, contradictory, changeable across time and place.) But I learned about using dictionaries to describe personalities by writing tag lines for romance novels and radio scripts in the early 1960s and 1970s.

I studied old-time radio from the 1930s and 1940s to find definitions of personality aspects, styles, and preferences that also appear in all types of dictionaries—from synonyms and thesauri, to rhyming dictionaries and books on action verbs. Then I looked at descriptions of character, position, and attitude as applied to corporations that reflected the personalities of their leaders. Many personality definitions and descriptions are found in the resumes I wrote for clients in the 1960s. Some of the best sources of personality definitions or descriptions include plays, scripts, novels, and poems.

Psychologists who design personality tests often go to these primary sources instead of the secondary sources (such as books by other psychoanalysts) because descriptions, tag lines, and dialogue contain definitions that read as portraits. This is because they are based on conversation broken down to the simplest parts of speech: descriptive words for people's preferences, decisions, and actions.

For example, is a person grounded, traditional, and routine, or imaginative, change-oriented, and creative? What kind of person is labeled as a conformist or a conventional, practical, detail-oriented thinker? What kind of individual is tagged as a sentimental, empathetic, abstract, theoretician with spiritual depth who never forgets names or birthdays? All these definitions of personality are based on water-cooler gossip or person-to-person, intimate conversation about someone's behavior under stress. Test design of personality assessments is about describing visual portraits of personalities.

I used to write and edit resumes, and help people describe themselves in essays, memoirs, books, or novels. Clients who asked for resumes, essays, or novels to be edited or written usually were eager to find a good match between the "character"—a position or attitude of specific corporations or editors—and the client's own personality styles. Matching people to corporations or editors is similar to matching single people seeking life partners. The key to designing a personality assessment is to find specific vivid "tag" words to express nuances and preferences chosen from a palette of personalities.

When writing novels and plays, I described emotions, behavior, and personality traits by painting visual portraits with definitions of behavior described by specific words. A person just didn't say something; he or she spoke the words "timorously," or "scoured with disdain in a voice dark as pumice," or "said yes marvelously," or expressed shyness by gazing at his sneakers. Those aspects of personality were called tag lines. The words had to describe the behavior and not the emotion. I design personality tests by noting and describing behavior and not emotion. It's the body language and the gestures that design the test. This is accomplished by finding the words that show the gestures or the behavior.

What's great about using dictionaries and thesauri to design personality assessments is how simple it is to design a test based on a dictionary definition of a personality trait, style, attribute, mood, texture, or preference. If you look at dictionaries throughout the world, each language has a word describing some aspect of personality, behavior, preference, or attitude.

The more words you find in a dictionary describing an aspect of personality, the more important that certain aspect of personality is to the specific society and language. That's why I designed tests based on how important and highly valued aspects of personality are based on the number of words ascribed to that particular trait.

I searched through dictionaries in English, French, German, Russian, Spanish, Italian, and Portuguese. Then I looked at how some Asian languages list words that are ascribed to certain personality traits. I looked at synonyms and antonyms.

If you want to design a personality test, go to the roots: Roget's Thesaurus, or any unabridged dictionary. Scientists already have searched dictionaries and thesauri for words describing aspects of character and personality continuously since and during the 19th and mid-20th centuries. (Look up names such as Gordon Allport, American psychologist of the mid-20th century, and Francis Galton,

19th-century British scientist, two scientists mentioned in Annie Murphy Paul's book, *The Cult of Personality*.) Scientists go to dictionaries to define personality traits because they are looking for the simplest definition. And who creates those definitions? Mostly people gossiping about how various people act and speak towards strangers or relatives who don't have the power to hire, pay, or promote them.

In my opinion, personality tests given by corporations should emphasize simplicity. Employers buying corporate tests based on validity and value really are buying easy-to-follow, step-by-step clarity also known as simplicity.

Simplicity in a personality test means the assessment gives you all the answers you were looking for in your life in exotic places, but found it close by. Employers are not supposed to ever hire or fire based on personality test results. Employers want to hire and promote those who pose the least financial risk to the corporation.

Therefore, a simple personality test should tell the employer what traits an individual has that allow the person to stand on his or her own two feet and put bread on the table. That's the moral point of any personality test, to pull your own weight, and *pulling your own weight* is a buzz phrase that personality assessments measure through simplicity. There are no right or wrong answers, only individual differences.

Personality testing is the backbone of HR departments. Personality tests emphasize morals, confidence, self-insight, empathy, emotional maturity, traits, job interest preferences, and universal values that hold true for everyone. If you score a certain way on a personality test, you create "buzz appeal" or charisma, provided that what you score matches the character of the corporation's leaders and/or founders.

Corporate tests are all about how you differ from others on your team at work. Although employers should not hire based on personality tests, and you're not supposed to have "wrong" answers, personality test results are used to measure commitment, reliability, and responsibility. Emotional quotient tests are relied on to assess empathy and maturity.

Simply put, to pass a corporate personality test, your answers should have some redemptive value to a universal audience. That's the most important point: Personality profiling tests give you the momentum to move along the pipeline, leading to all the right connections from team-building to decision-making. Expected test answers should show that you'll do the best you can do under the circumstances and that you trust in your self-insight. Decision-making tests point out what obstacles you need to overcome in a reduced amount of time and what blind spots, such as valuable details, you overlooked that could derail your career.

Without the "buzz appeal" of personality test results, you might not get the attention you deserve at work. Corporate tests help you from falling through the cracks. No matter how great your work is, unless you find someone to "buzz" you into the eyes of your employer, you might not be noticed that easily.

The results have to be presented at the right time just when your expertise and experience is "in vogue" with your company. If someone is looking for personality profiles, decision-making test results, or tests of emotional maturity similar to your results, enough tests can "buzz you in."

Look at the value of the test. Does it hold any weight with your employer? Is the test simple enough for you to follow? Simple is understandable, and that's the buzz right now in tests. A test has value only when it is judged simple and earthy in the news and print media.

On a personality test, you have to be yourself. Assessments can spot phoniness in a minute. Be true to yourself. Personality tests are about your traits, interest inventories, and preferences.

Your test results are judged by what is valuable to your boss. So tests must ask you simple questions, and you need to answer simply. Tests go through fads, just as book genres do, every few years. But commitment to your company, self-insight, and hindsight are universal values. Target those values on a test.

What answers give you the most credibility among your peers and employers, and are true to yourself? Employers are impressed by tests that symbolize stability, dependability, security, and centeredness. Those are universal values corporations want to see in employees at all levels. Test results give you visibility and credibility if you're a match with the corporate leader's employment needs and match the "personality aspects" of the corporation's philosophy, purpose, and goals.

Corporate testing gives you a voice of resilience, hindsight, and self-scrutiny. You can develop insight into your dominant personality traits because surviving the corporate world depends upon internal scrutiny. Personality testing motivates you to examine your drives and differences with the goal of refining your triumphs.

Employers Test Personality to See How Employees Deal With Conflicts

The corporate world is intense. Corporate assessments are designed to help us make sense of a person's ability to handle problems. Employers need to know how their staff deals with conflicts within corporate.

The purpose of personality profiling and decision-making testing is to find what blind spots exist in a person (such as overlooking important details under the pressures of reduced time) when making decisions that can derail careers.

There's a new trend in corporate testing called the *bio-inventory*. Assessments in the corporate world are given to see how individual differences shape corporate teams. Testing develops insight. Assessments are guides to avoiding pitfalls. Personality testing allows you to define who you are in a job-related context by showing you how you take information in, process it, and make decisions.

Personality assessments offer rich portraits of how employees under stress, and under normal corporate conditions, deal with conflicts, solve problems, and arrive at results. Corporate assessments offer rare glimpses into the inner worlds of workers. Corporate testing results, when interpreted in depth, also can give workers guidelines, confidence, recognition, and a voice of leadership.

Business leaders need reliable *systems* to validate concepts. Results must be tangible, measurable, and easy to follow. To maintain marketability, executives require a system of proactive steps. Employers are looking for confidence, endurance, and resilience in workers. Employees at all levels want recognition, a greater sense of self, and a voice.

Employers care how you make sense of the world because your employer wants you to be reliable—as reliable as the test. You're hired because you pose the least financial risk to your employer.

Most corporations don't use personality tests for job selection. Instead, they use job-related skills tests, including tests to screen out angry, disruptive, and/or dishonest job applicants, and abilities tests. Usually, executives and managers are given team-building assessments and tests of decision-making abilities, including personality assessments.

What You Will Learn in This Book

After reading this book, you will learn:

1. What positive attitudes employers want to see on personality assessments and profiling, including tests of preference, interests, honesty, anger management, and disruptiveness.

2. How to solve problems, get results, and simplify answers for clarity that others can follow step by step on questionnaires and essay questions relating to creativity.

3. What your legal rights are when taking corporate personality assessments.

4. How to ace team-building and leadership assessments under stress and under normal corporate conditions by avoiding the blind spots that derail executive careers early on.

Anne Hart
Sacramento, California

$?$ $?$ $?$ $?$ $?$ $?$ $?$ $?$

Introduction

What Results Employers Want to See on a Personality Test

When employers consider your personality test results, they are looking for your ability to connect with others and communicate clearly. Being misunderstood in communication is one of the main reasons for conflict in the workplace. That's why personality assessments are given by corporations—to see how you connect with others and to measure whether you pose the least financial risk to your potential employer.

Certain types of job descriptions don't want a creative, artistic, bubbly personality in jobs that require adaptability to routine, accuracy, and speed. Other job descriptions want creativity within a set of company rules coupled with the ability to persuade, sell, motivate, inspire, train co-workers, and attract customers while focusing on amplifying the company's image, purpose, and growth goals.

Connecting with co-workers and managers is the secondary reason you're hired or promoted. The hidden primary reason you're hired or promoted is a financial one. You pose the least financial risk, whether it be in insurance, accommodation, or simply on your potential based on credentials, experience, and certification.

When a personality test is "confidential" and is sealed in your permanent records, it may be treated as a medical record (that is, open only to an insurance company). Or a personality test is passed around human resources and discussed with your employer. It depends upon the specific assessment. A test of honesty/integrity/loyalty would be brought to the attention of your employer.

A test of personality preference might arouse interest if your personality choices and behavior had no relation to the specific duties of the job. For example, if you're an artistic personality in search of free creativity reign in computer game design, and the job description calls for transcribing medical records from digital or tape recordings into text, why would you be hired before a person who prefers a more conventional job?

Employers who do get to see your personality test results are looking for a history of behavior desirable in workplace settings. Above all you need to connect to management and co-workers. Your personality test results and behavior in real time are a corridor, a route, and are looked upon as a passageway or gallery through which the image and reputation of your place of employment or corporation passes.

Personality testing acts as a conveyor belt: You're passed along when you merge, when you don't stand out. And at the same time you must stand out in such a way that it increases company production, lessens risk, and increases revenue. A personality test is a connection, link, nexus, anchor, and bridge between you and any potential a corporation offers if you use behavior to connect customers with the company. You're the point at which strangers and the corporation connects.

That's why behavior is a tool to be spliced by coaches, human resources managers, and talent. Personality assessments turn behavior into commitments of values. What behavior do employers want to see on a personality survey? They want to see your personality and workplace behavior described as you would review a good restaurant: brisk, accurate service, appropriate good taste, and sociability.

You must connect with the employer, but it must be done in a warm, friendly manner. Simple modesty goes a long way. If the answers fall in place as to preferences, you are ready to start team-building skills. But are you executive material? You are if you fit the description of a good restaurant from the previous paragraph. After all, your behavior is a mirror representing a refection of your company's image, potential for growth, and reputation.

？ ？ ？ ？ ？ ？ ？ ？

Chapter 1

Why Corporations Administer Tests, and Who Offers Them

In the last 30 years, the use of personality assessments and a wide variety of psychological tests has dramatically increased in the corporate environment. Building better teams, training executives to improve leadership skills, and testing job applicants for honesty and loyalty, while screening out potentially disruptive individuals, are some reasons for giving personality assessments.

Job applicants in medium-sized to large corporations in the past were tested in job-related skills performance such as mechanical ability, typing speed, accuracy, and yet at the same time the test publishers insisted that personality questionnaires are not to be used for hiring or termination.

20 Questions and Answers

1. Why do corporations administer personality tests?

Personality tests are given for three reasons. First, they're given so the corporation hires the employee who poses the least financial risk to the corporation. A second reason is to find ways to improve decision-making skills under reduced time pressure among executives and to improve team-building strategies. A third reason is to help cut down measurable increasing violence in the workplace by better screening.

Employers are afraid of hiring liars, bullies, and loose cannons who can't connect with other workers, fit into the group, make good decisions under pressure, or work well with teams. Whereas corporations are expected by law to hire and accommodate people with disabilities if they can do the required job tasks, employers don't want disruptive, violent people in the workplace. The trouble is corporate testing can't screen out the potentially violent business partners.

A sore point is whether to hire a troubled worker who put on the charm at work but could turn violent under pressure in the future. The key word is *could*. Corporations want to cut risk and increase assurance with employees. Employees want to feel safe with fellow co-workers.

Employers need a flawless system with time-tested rules to screen and train workers at all levels. Test designers have a mission: to build into tests alarms that recognize "lies" on the answer sheets.

The exordial and sometimes hidden reasons for giving certain types of personality profiling, integrity, and anger assessments is that some corporate questionnaires with built-in "lie" alarms may help screen out potentially disruptive, angry, dishonest, or violent employees without the test-taker knowing it.

Corporations want to withdraw attention to screening out bullies that assault and focus on testing for self-insight and honesty. Employers care how workers solve conflicts. Increased insurance premiums can occur when a worker harasses or intimidates other workers and that worker's action causes harm.

Workplace violence is on the upswing. According to the U.S. Bureau of Labor Statistic's 2005 census, one out of five deaths in the workplace was caused by assaults or self-inflicted injuries in California. Eighty-seven people in California died in 2005 from violent acts in the workplace, up significantly from 52 in 2004, according to a census of fatal workplace injuries from the U.S. Bureau of Labor Statistics. Can corporate personality questionnaires help prevent some types of workplace violence? Corporations administer personality assessments indirectly to help prevent injuries on the job due to anger-management problems.

The ultimate goal of the assessment is to find out how employees can avoid conflict and miscommunication by seeking self-insight from the testing. At the same time a test should help save time and increase production levels, revenues, and employee turnover, including downtime due to employee conflicts.

Human resources personnel, coaches, psychologists, and instructional designers call corporate personality tests "assessments." Tests of honesty or integrity usually are referred to as "personality surveys." These types of assessments also can be labeled questionnaires, indicators, classifiers, sorters, or profilers. All of them have several goals in common: to provide self-insight, explore values, and reveal habits of how people take in information, process data, and make decisions.

2. Who offers corporate assessments?

Large companies, institutions, schools, the military, and the government as well as large retailers and temporary services often give corporate assessments, ranging from job skills and abilities assessments to personality questionnaires.

3. What kind of corporate tests are given?

Personality assessments and profiles, decision-making tests, tests of cognitive intelligence or critical thinking, and creativity tests usually are given. Some personality surveys include tests of integrity/honesty and may include questionnaires to screen out angry, potentially disruptive job applicants from the corporate workplace.

Other tests may be related to leadership and team-building skills, such as avoiding blind spots by overlooking important details before making decisions that might derail an executive early on in the individual's career. Physical endurance exams are given for some jobs, general health exams for others, and exams for drugs for still other jobs. Some personality assessments also include questionnaires to select career or job-related interest niche areas, such as a preference for creative or artistic work, routine work, clerical work, academic work, or realistic work.

4. To whom are the tests given? Managers? Job applicants?

Tests are given to job applicants and managers. Executives take personality tests to develop and improve specific blind spots in their leadership skills or decision-making habits. Most personality tests in corporate settings are used for team-building, and the tests may be given by coaches, instructional designers, or members of the HR department. In retail settings, tests of honesty may be scored by computers but given by retail managers or human resources department supervisors and managers.

5. Why do corporations place so much emphasis on tests?

Employers test all levels of workers to see how they deal with conflicts, solve problems, perform specific job skills, and obtain results or answers that increase production and pose the least financial risk to the company. An exception is the cost of accommodation for people with disabilities. Personality assessments provide self-insight into revealing behavior such as impatience.

Business leaders need reliable systems to validate concepts. Results must be tangible, measurable, and easy to follow. To maintain marketability, executives require a system of proactive steps. Employers are looking for confidence, endurance, and resilience in workers.

6. What should you look for in a test?

Make sure you know what your rights are and that questions on a test relate specifically to the type of work or job description you'll be doing and are not about your personal life outside the workplace. Look for questions that help guide you to the best-fit job niche or the best way to make decisions under stress.

Most personality questionnaire responses are looking for normal responses, what is polite in a corporate setting. Empathy is important. Put yourself in the other person's place and respond in a way that demonstrates how you'd like to be treated in a work setting. Look for clarity and expert, relatively flawless validation in a test.

The questions should be specific and not vague or ambiguous. Simple answers that are clear to understand are best. Be honest, and don't try to trick the test, because most tests have built-in lie detectors that sound the alarm. In a general personality test, your goal is to match your personality with the character traits and "vision" of the corporation's present leaders for your specific job duties and for the firm's growth plans.

Companies have two types of character traits: traditional or forward-looking. They are either change-oriented or rely on imitating successful, larger corporations where rules have worked well in the past and are still working. They will look for people who fit into their philosophy.

7. What's the difference between personality, creativity, job-interest category, and abilities tests?

A personality assessment is a questionnaire that lets you choose what character trait feels most comfortable or best fits your actions, interests, and responses. It's an assessment of self-insight. A creativity test lets you apply your imagination to solve real problems that get results. A job-interest category is a questionnaire of your specific interests in job descriptions and duties. An abilities test shows you how well you perform in critical thinking, reading comprehension, cognitive intelligence, job skills, or any other specific ability, such as clerical aptitude.

8. How do personality tests differ from abilities tests?

Personality assessments have no right or wrong answers. They are designed to give you self-insight into what your preferences are. Do you make decisions quickly or take a lot of time to make sure you don't overlook important details? Abilities tests measure reasoning, comprehension, or job skills.

Personality questionnaires are about insight, values, and integrity. They also may include hobby-type interests. The purpose is to find out what you really enjoy doing with your time. Personality assessments measure how you take in information, use the information, and make decisions. Abilities tests are about *performance* in specific skills. Some abilities tests measure critical thinking and/ or abstract reasoning, mechanical, numerical, or spatial abilities. Other abilities tests measure reading comprehension skills.

9. What do abilities and personality tests measure?

Abilities tests measure skills, reasoning, or aptitude. Personality assessments measure values, self-insight, and career or hobby interests. Integrity questionnaires measure honesty or loyalty. Job-task inventories measure career-related preferences. Other tests measure anger management, behavior, or decision-making.

10. How are abilities measured?

Abilities are measured by tests of achievement, advanced placement, critical thinking, abstract reasoning, clerical reasoning, specific subject performance, job-related skills performance, reading comprehension, verbal ability, analogies, or other verbal, mathematical, spatial, or mechanical tests that measure performance and skills, usually related to the job or to critical thinking and reasoning.

There may also be tests for leadership skills and abilities, or for decision-making abilities where what is measured is a peer-evaluated agreement on what constitutes a "good" decision or "good" leadership skills in that particular corporation. Other leadership abilities tests may be generalized and apply to any type of business.

Leadership abilities include being outgoing and having easy-to-understand speaking ability. Peers also need to describe you as being somewhat charismatic or enthusiastic about a subject while speaking or writing. Leadership ability also depends upon motivating people to follow your facts and reasoning backed up by motivational enthusiasm.

11. Where are the results applied in an employment situation?

Test results are filed in an employee's permanent record in a corporation's human resources department or in a special file set aside for test results.

12. How can you prepare to take corporate personality tests?

Make sure your biorhythms are relaxed and not under stress. Get rest, be alert, and eat balanced meals. Take the practice tests in this book and learn what the employer expects of you on the job and what is expected of you on the test.

Know what your legal rights are regarding answering personal questions. Are the questions related to job performance, behavior, specialized skills, or personality and general interest preferences? Various federal and state lows protect the rights and the privacy of all prospective employees. Before administering personality tests, employers determine the legal limits of their testing. Generally, the tests cannot discriminate because of race, color, religion, sex, or national origin. The Americans with Disabilities Act (ADA) prohibits inquiring into mental illness, so the tests measure personality, not psychological abnormalities.

Understand how to take the test, and be honest. Know enough about yourself so that you have self-insight. Look over sample tests for foresight, insight, and hindsight. Learn what pitfalls to avoid by reading about the test and finding out whether your personality matches closely with that of the leaders in your corporation in regard to their goals for the company.

If you're forward-looking and the company is traditional, is there a job for you with that company that allows you to be change-oriented? Or will your job be routine for many decades? The best way to prepare for a personality assessment is to find out through research whether your personality matches the character traits of the corporation's leaders and supervisors in your department.

13. Who scores the tests?

Personality questionnaires may be self-scored, scored by computers, or sent away for scoring to the test publisher's psychometrics division. Or they may be scored by the human resources department of your corporation. Some tests are scored by instructional designers, by outsourced coaches, or by organizational, industrial, and social psychologists hired by the company as consultants or clients.

14. What do the scores mean or how are they applied?

Scores on personality questionnaires usually are represented by alphabetical letters or words that symbolize your dominant personality style. There are no right or wrong answers, only self-insight gained by understanding how the assessments are interpreted. Look for detailed rather than generalized interpretations. Explanations may be given instead of numerical scores. The point is not to see how high your score is, but what personality traits dominate the way you prefer to observe, process information, and make decisions. Personality assessments measure what you choose to reveal that are the most comfortable paths for you to take in dealing with choices. An example is whether you prefer to plan ahead or be surprised.

These letters or words that describe your dominant personality preferences simply tell you what ways of responding you favor. You answer the questions by selecting what feels most comfortable, most like the "real" you.

15. How do the scores influence whether you'll be hired or promoted?

You're not supposed to be hired or promoted from a personality test, as it has no bearing on your job skills or performance. It's about self-insight on what responses feel most healthy and pose the least wear and tear on your body and mind in the long run.

The purpose of a personality test also is to screen out dishonest, disruptive potential employees from a pool of job applicants. Personality tests also let you match your preferences and goals with the preferences and goals of the leaders of your corporation.

Any personality can do most any type of job, but outgoing people may be energized, engaged, and remain in a joyous mood longer in a job that requires constant talking with people face to face, whereas reflective people who enjoy working alone may become stressed, impatient, and tired by constant daily face-to-face contact with people who need information quickly. The personality assessment is designed to find out what type of activity frustrates you the most—working alone or working face-to-face with people. There's another factor: time flexibility in work versus rigid, company-set time requirements.

A personality assessment helps match what feels healthy to you with the actual tasks of your job on a long-term daily basis. Personality tests influence you because they are about self-insight, behavior, and choice.

Your test responses may change from day to day unless you really know yourself and what feels comfortable for you. It's all about self-insight, foresight, and hindsight, and about finding your own pitfalls to avoid.

Your scores will influence your job only if your employer wants the same personality style as himself/herself. Legally, you're not supposed to be hired or fired by the results of a personality test that has no relation to job skills and no wrong answers. However, tests of honesty, certain values, or anger are often used to screen out angry, potentially disruptive job applicants or disturbed people. How well do you connect with your co-workers? What do they think of you? All these considerations can be compared by looking at differences on personality tests between you, your employers, and your co-workers. Your employer really wants to screen out people who are troubled and/or problematic from his or her corporation, along with bullies and people filled with rage directed at co-workers and those with problems and habits that distract from their ability to do the job well and on time. Personality tests may be given to help prevent violence in the workplace. You're hired when you can connect with the group and fit in with the rest of the workers, in addition to posing the least financial risk to the employer.

16. What do personality tests measure?

Personality assessments measure choice, preference, values, behavior, decisions, attitudes, integrity, and general or job-related interests.

17. What good are decision-making tests?

They help you avoid blind spots due to overlooked details. Reduced time pressure with increased information affects decision-making ability. The problem is that the time allowed to make decisions at work is rapidly decreasing as the amount of information coming in to corporations is increasing. Training in making good and quicker decisions is provided to find middle ground. How do you decide under increasing pressure? You learn to prioritize and multitask in improved ways.

18. Why do test results vary for day to day?

Answers given under stress may vary at different times, moods, and attitudes. That's why your score on personality tests will change unless you really know yourself (self-insight training).

19. Who decides how good your decisions are?

Peers, coaches, and employers decide whether your decisions are good based on whether all important details were considered under the pressure and stress of reduced time. If important information or values were overlooked and decisions made too hastily, it can be an indication of future poor decision-making.

Coaches and consultants, human relations managers, instructional designers, or organizational psychologists may be hired as consultants to train managers in team-building and decision-making as well as administer personality profiling tests to discern leadership skills followed up by training in decision-making and leadership.

20. For what main reasons are you hired or promoted?

When you pose the least financial risk to and connect with your employer, your co-workers, and your division manager's growth vision and present image of the company. You'll be hired if your job skills meet the requirements of the job, and your personality traits make comfortable matches with the character traits of the corporation's leaders. You're also hired if your age and health aren't factors with co-workers and employers.

?

The new trend is the bio-inventory. It blurs boundaries between personality profiling and cognitive abilities testing.

It's a variation on personality profiling currently used to evaluate learning strategies across institutions. Originally, the bio-inventory assessed teaching and learning in biology.

After "being implemented" in the corporate world, the bio-inventory currently is used to assess the effectiveness of many different types of tutorials as learning tools. Corporate assessments can be designed to test almost anything that can be measured and validated. The bio-inventory and other applications from academia are increasingly being adapted and used in corporate testing. The last instrument an employer wants is a test that hasn't been validated and reviewed as reliable.

Assessments such as the bio-inventory, job simulation, and culture-free tests appeal to corporate leaders because such tests rely on systems that have gone through many implementations and iterations. The test adaptation process resembles technical documentation publishing. The following sample bio-inventory test is not only a test of knowledge but also is a tutorial. The words on the test can be about personality traits or about a specific subject or combine both fields.

The terminology can have a built-in personality classifier. Those with enough interest in the subject will take the time to look up word meanings in a glossary provided with the test of the terminology. Any subject matter can be included in a hybrid tutorial that could combine learning tools with personality assessments or with knowledge of specific job-related terminology, as in my medical terminology assessment and tutorial, which appears in Appendix H.

Various bio-inventory tests, which also are tutorials, contain fields that go through revisions prior to being published for corporate use. New applications are constantly being found for tests. Assessments that have been measured, validated, and reviewed in classrooms are adapted for corporate use for a good reason.

These tests appeal to executives because the assessments went through many editions within the system and are very reliable. They appeal to managers who "go by the book." To make a test more useful, it can be designed as a learning tutorial. Why learn only about a subject or its terminology when you also can learn about your personality, interests, or choice of a career at the same time?

It's all about benchmarking—relying on tradition, what worked in the past, and imitating successful giants. If it works, it doesn't need to be fixed. That's why assessments that historically fit into *systems* appeal to corporate leaders. They work. Tests successfully used in schools can be adapted for corporations. Even benchmarking needs a new take, a fresh new angle for learning to extend its usefulness.

That's why one of the newest trends in corporate testing is using the bio-inventory test that doubles as a learning tutorial. These new trends even put a learning curve and a fresh spin on traditional testing. Bio-inventory tutorials have two uses in the corporate world: imparting job-related knowledge and self-insight at the same time.

Testing How Employees Deal With Conflicts

Does the corporation shape peoples lives? Or do individual differences shape corporate teams?

Do personality and ability assessments offer rich portraits of how employees deal with conflict? Are corporate assessments rare glimpses into the inner worlds of workers? Does corporate testing give workers confidence, recognition, and a voice?

Does testing create too much drama in the workplace? Is there a place at work for new rhythms within applications that deal with people instead of products? Is testing counterintuitive? Or does testing find the blind spots?

How does corporate testing allow you to define who you are in a job-related context? And why is it important to a corporation? Why does your boss care how you make sense of the world? Your boss cares because your employer wants you to be reliable—as reliable as the test.

Honesty Assessments

Many of the larger retail corporations give job applicants an honesty assessment, often called a test of integrity. Other assessments are self-report questionnaires on values used in dealing with day-by-day decisions.

Measuring values could include honesty, equality, attitudes, diversity issues, independence, social smarts, and emotional maturity. Some assessments that look for values answers and give training as a follow-up are usually given to managers, but also may be given to a wide variety of employees, such as at a seminar on how to deal with diversity in the workplace.

Other types of questionnaires may cover motivation. In the job-selection process, assessments that measure motivation are common. Employers want to assess the depth and breadth of interest in the job tasks. If a test shows you're not motivated, you probably would not be selected for that job or task.

According to the National Workrights Institute (*www.workrights.org/ issue_other/oi_statement_3-26-90.html*), about "15 [percent] of all companies currently use honesty tests. These 5000 companies administer about 2.5 million tests annually. They are generally used as a pre-employment screen by retail firms concerned about employee theft."

Wal-Mart gives job applicants a personality survey that contains multiple-choice questions relating to honesty. You can read more about Wal-Mart's personality survey and questions on integrity in Barbara Ehrenreich's 2001 bestseller, *Nickel and Dimed*. Ehrenreich took the personality survey at Wal-Mart, as she reports in her book about what it's like working at entry-level jobs that pay at or close to the minimum wage.

According to the National Workrights Institute, in 2005, when a new Wal-Mart store opened in Oakland, California, 11,000 people applied for only 400 job openings. Assessments sometimes symbolize or reflect the strength or weakness of the entire labor market.

An article at the National Workrights Institute site noted that, in a boom hiring market, retailers sometimes increase wages to recruit more people. In a weaker labor market, people will line up to apply for what jobs are available. If it's a seller's market in labor, stress assessments may be used more often to find out how workers can improve their motivation by increasing energy based on better health.

Stress Assessments

Developing *hardiness* to stress at all levels is important for corporations. That's why professionals with expertise in specialized occupations often give assessments followed up by training in stress-reduction techniques.

Leslie Furlow, RN, Ph.D., president of AchieveMentors, Inc., an interim management service of ManageMentors in Cleburne, Texas, provides consulting and development to the healthcare industry. Her corporation administers the **DiSC**, **Hardiness**, and **Stress** tools assessments. She said in an e-mail to Anne Hart:

> There is no preparation for taking the test. That would invalidate the assessment. We do the DiSC, Hardiness, and Stress tools. We are working to develop hardiness in management. The assessment gives us a base line to evaluate the development process. The results are interpreted using standard research methodology. Usually a member of the executive team hires us. Since we work mostly with hospitals, the VP of Patient Care Services hires us to give these assessments. They can justify the

money they spend on corporate development. Testing should be used only when it has a purpose that will be applied to improve the individual or the corporation. Testing to eliminate people should not be practiced.

What Do Corporate Tests Measure?

Tests measure reliability, but how reliable are the tests? If you want to test an assessment's reliability, you repeat the identical test again in a few days and compare your scores.

Corporate tests usually measure and evaluate the following: honesty (integrity), anger management, entrepreneurial aptitude, stress tolerance, leadership, cognitive intelligence abilities (IQ), emotional maturity, personality preference and profiling, extroversion, aptitudes, attitudes (race relations or beliefs), blind spots (whether you overlook information), decision-making ability, neuroticism, performance, speed in recognizing individual differences, openness, reliability, conscientiousness, and agreeableness.

Corporate tests also include interest classifiers or subject area questionnaires. Topics of interest include different types of communication styles, decision-making, problem-solving, mechanical dexterity, negotiating, forecasting, analyzing, and organizing either data, objects, or people.

For job applicants, tests also consist of measurements of job skills, reading comprehension, numerical skills, clerical practice, editing/proofreading, manual dexterity, and grammar/spelling. Executives are given more personality assessments than entry-level applicants, but entry-level applicants take more tests of integrity/honesty and job-skill performance, such as data entry keystroke speed.

Of all these factors, measuring decision-making ability and personality profile stand out in personality assessments when testing potential leaders, managers, and executives. Corporate testing for a particular trait is widely used to improve pre-hiring decisions.

To maintain marketability, executives require a system of proactive steps. Corporations want to know whether you use more or less of any particular aspect of your personality or abilities. There are between four and five thousand English-language ability tests on the market measuring abstract, verbal, numerical, perceptual, spatial, and mechanical reasoning, according to Mark Parkinson, Ph.D., a leading business psychologist. Parkinson is a psychometric test co-designer and author of numerous test-taking guidebooks, including *How to Master Psychometric Tests* and *How to Master Personality Questionnaires*. In addition to abilities assessments, there are personality classifiers. For further information on personality classifiers, see *Ace the Corporate Personality Test* by Edward Hoffman, Ph.D., a licensed clinical psychologist.

Determining Personality Preferences

Just as managers, executives, and scientists make a business of organizing to impose order on a corporation and its products or services, so do some assessments sort, classify, and categorize personalities. Published research is extensive on how many people of a particular personality category work in a specific occupation.

The search is on for reliable systems that can reduce each part of personality to its purest label. Personality preference product merchandising even offers mugs, tee shirts, brooches and other memorabilia with your own Jungian type or temperament letters. (See the Paladin Myers-Briggs Online Store at *www.paladinexec/store/*. The Website announces, "Welcome to Paladin Associates Online Store™. Don't keep it a secret! Show the world! Display your personality on Paladin's uniquely designed tee shirt highlighting your individual personality type characteristics. Select your type from the table below to view your picture and to place your order. If you know the personality type of friends or family members these tee shirts make excellent presents.")

Personality-related cartoons may be purchased from the Cartoon Stock Website *www.cartoonstock.com/directory/p/personality_types_gifts.asp*. Pictures of Personality Typology.Net offers a personality type TV show online (*www.typology.net/typetvshow/*). According to the site, "The Type TV Show takes you behind the scenes, and shows you what is under the costumes and games people play."

Using Dictionaries to Define Personality and Character Traits

In order to develop a system executives can use in a corporate setting to measure personality, scientists turned to dictionaries and several types of thesaurr. For more information on the history of personality assessments, see Annie Murphy Paul's 2004 book, *The Cult of Personality*.

You can read a brief history of the search to find personality through looking at language (and the scientists) in Paul's book. The idea is that if a part of personality can be defined, there will be a word for it. The theory is called "lexical hypothesis."

If early researchers historically looked at dictionaries and thesauri, how many more definitions of personality might have been defined in languages other than English? Perhaps some other language or culture has a word for character or attitude that doesn't appear in English. After all, people who live in Arctic latitudes have more words for snow than appear in English, there are more words for shapes of pasta in Italy than in England, and more words for courage in Amerindian. Why not more words for personality aspects in another language or another system—such as subatomic physics, math, molecular genetics, or chemistry?

Assessments Used as Interventions

Coaches are hired for their insight into revealing blind spots. Coaches are brought into companies to use interventions that impact specific job-related behaviors. Because people differ, coaches are trained and hired to recognize "blind spots" that "lead to executive derailment," as pointed out in course announcements from the IPAT (Institute for Personality and Ability Testing) Website (*www.ipat.com/*). A coach 'intervenes' in a company's human resources business much the same way as a consulting engineer, chemist, or architect is called in to solve a product-related problem.

The assessment is used as an intervention tool. Assessments allow coaches, teams, and executives to consider alternative ways to solve people problems in order to increase productivity. A coach is hired to show people who differ in personality how they can solve problems with efficacy by working together by becoming aware of the blind spots. It's all about foresight, insight, hindsight, and studying pitfalls to avoid.

What Types of Intelligence Do You Use at Work?

Many personality assessments seem to be based on specific traits. Your boss wants to define and measure your character, identity, and independence on a scale.

Corporations, schools, and the government not only want to measure how intelligent you are. They now want to know what types of intelligence you use in different workplace roles.

How do you score on social smarts or emotional intelligence? In 1995, Daniel Goleman wrote a book titled *Emotional Intelligence: Why It Can Matter More than IQ*. Then, in 2006, Karl Albrecht wrote a book titled *Social Intelligence: The New Science of Success*. Some corporations give emotional quotient assessments in addition to intelligence tests and personality tests to measure how you experience what Goleman calls your "social radar."

EQ—that is, emotional quotient—tests your emotional maturity. Some tests measure whether you can postpone gratification. Other EQ tests how you treat people and how well you connect in business to the team, or to co-workers and management. Emotionally, are you executive material, or more suited to be an entrepreneur?

Social Smarts

Corporate assessments often measure how you use social intelligence to connect to people. Emotional intelligence tests reveal how you use empathy (that is, people smarts) as a catalyst to bring together unrelated details, corporations, institutions, agencies, and individuals in specific job roles to solve a problem at work (or in life).

Social intelligence measures how you observe, simplify, and offer commitment. EQ also is defined by some as charisma and by others as empathy. Actually, it's emotional maturity.

What all these personality assessments have in common is that they might be used by a corporation to determine whether or not you fit into the group. The wheel must run smoothly, supported by the spokes, so the company can move forward. Employees don't come from the same cookie-cutter mold.

If you fit in the group, you're more likely to fit on the team, even though the team is made up of different personality styles that somehow *connect*. In a world made of different cookie-cutters, you still have to fit into the group.

The person who best connects to the group fits into an already-cut jigsaw puzzle slot (the corporation). Jigsaw puzzle pieces are made up of different shapes, but they still fit into a mold, an already-cut-out place that matches the shape of each piece. That's how you fit into the group: by connecting. Social smarts assessments measure and evaluate you on how you connect to others.

Fitting Into the Team

The more extreme the transitional age (the age when younger members are identified and groomed to replace senior employees), the more passionately corporations seek to define identity from their teams. The corporations' goal is simple: they intend to maintain the health of their executives and keep insurance costs down, the risk low, and the bottom-line profit up. Whatever happens in the home reverberates at work. Corporate testing maintains that correct personality and identity they want in an executive, which are both genetic and cultural in nature.

Extroversion and introversion are biological and can be tested by measuring how much saliva is excreted under stress. Introverts feel higher stress when working rapidly in a group under the pressure of decreasing time constraints. They will secrete more saliva than extroverts doing the same tasks in the same time allowed.

When it comes to sports celebrities, it's not trait assessments that are given. Instead, tests of cognitive ability are administered on the belief that if a test-taking tutor can improve your score on an intelligence test, then, as your thought processes advance, so will your athletic reaction.

Why Corporations Give the Wonderlic Test to Job Applicants

The Wonderlic Personnel Test (*www.wonderlic.com*) is a 12-minute test of problem-solving skills, or cognitive ability, given widely to job applicants. According to a June 30, 2005, press release for the revised Wonderlic Personnel Test (WPT-R), titled "Final Field-Testing for Wonderlic's WPT-R," the test has been taken by more than 125 million job applicants since its release in 1937.

The Wonderlic Personnel Test (WPT) has been used in employee selection by more than 10,000 organizations. Popularly known for its use in the National Football League (NFL) draft, the WPT is a mainstay at organizations in virtually all industries, many of whom participated in the 2005 field study.

Executives usually are not given job skills tests that measure knowledge of computer operation, programming, data entry, or keyboarding speeds. Those are given to entry-level workers along with math and reading comprehension tests, or to people who program computers and work with databases or medical records administration, according to the June 30, 2005, Wonderlic press release.

According to a 2006 sports piece by staff writer Pat Sangimini, posted on the Website for KMBCTV, Kansas City (*www.thekansascitychannel.com/sports/517714/detail.html*) titled "Leaf's Fallen—But Can He Get Back Up?," National Football League (NFL) teams gave the Wonderlic intelligence test to players. Sangimino's article notes, "The Wonderlic test has become a staple of the combine." (The article actually spells Wonderlic as "Wunderlick.") According to the article, ironically, the Wonderlic test measures reading skills. Fifty questions have to be answered in 12 minutes. Why does the National Football League rely so much on the Wonderlic test—a test of intelligence? If the Wonderlic test is being used "to screen which football players to draft, trade and sign," then those who manage football players often hire test coaches to "tutor" the football players in how to best ace an intelligence test such as the Wonderlic.

Sangimino's piece details how one agent (Leigh Steinberg) "hired a test-taking coach" for a client (Akili Smith) two years before the football draft. The article gives the before and after scores, names a few players, and also reports that the client doubled his score from his previous Wonderlic score.

Why are NFL teams spending more money on intelligence testing? If higher Wonderlic scores appear to improve chances for a football player to get more money or negotiate a contract, then intelligence tests are about being chosen for a bigger piece of the pie. Testing then becomes associated with increasing commissions for the players if they score high.

What's really behind the battle for higher Wonderlic intelligence scores for the football players is the connection between improving athletic reaction time by getting tutoring in how to take an intelligence test.

Certain fast-thinking positions, such as quarterbacks, offensive linemen, and linebackers, can benefit by working to increase their scores on intelligence tests. The test coaches teach the football players how to take the test by having the players practice how to better understand the questions. It boils down to better getting tutored in reading comprehension. The results of the Wonderlic test become so important that the score could determine whether the player is or isn't drafted into the NFL.

Why should intelligence in reading or solving math problems be associated with reaction time in athletics? It works: The better you are on an intelligence test, the better your reaction time might be. Does this also hold true for reaction time while driving or responding quickly to crises events?

On the Wonderlic test, scoring runs from 1 to 50. According to Wonderlic, Inc., the average score for college students is around 25. Among the corporate and intelligence testing coaches who "tutor" sports contenders, it also has been said that anyone scoring on the Wonderlic test greater than 30 is considered sharp.

The Wonderlic test frequently is given to job applicants seeking administrative assistant work. Two decades ago, numerous temporary service agencies used to tell secretarial applicants they needed to have at least a score of 22 to be referred for temporary employment in general clerical work. Other job skills tests such as typing speed also were given to new job applicants.

Interestingly, the NFL quarterbacks are most likely to score above 30—after they've been coached in numerous cases. Wonderlic scores of NFL football players often are reported online on football fan Websites, as well as mentioned in sports articles on *ESPN.com* and *USAToday.com*.

Online, the discussion groups often repeat that the Wonderlic scores of certain football players currently run from 6 to 50. The players with a score of 6 are still playing football. So why is it so important if job selection doesn't always depend on your scores? In the corporate world, getting hired may depend upon whether your score on the Wonderlic meets the minimum requirements to be hired for general office work.

Corporate and intelligence testing coaches are being hired by some of the agents of football players and other sports professionals. What's not reported online are various celebrities' personality profiling "scores," or results of tests for anger management or disruptive behavior. When there are no wrong or right answers on personality assessments as there are on intelligence tests, there is little media interest in the personality preferences of sports figures or other celebrities.

Read Reviews Online of Commercially-Available Tests and Built-In Validity Checks

Be aware of the validity checks built into the instrument. Validity checks look for consistency in your answers. The validity checks work by *comparing* the consistency of your responses against what would be found with many other similar profiles, responses, or answers.

How can you tell whether that corporate assessment you'll be taking is flawed or dependable? Has your boss or your HR department director read all those online reviews of the assessments given to the staff? Because you're going to be taking these tests, it's a good idea to read reviews online of corporate assessments and other mental measurements.

Assessment reviews have their own Website. The Buros Institute of Mental Measurements, University of Nebraska-Lincoln(*www.unl.edu/buros/history.html*), provides "candidly critical" reviews of commercially available tests. As such, the Buros Institute of Mental Measurements offers a service to individuals seeking to find out about the development, standardization, reliability, and validity of many testing instruments currently in use by various organizations. You also can read online about its services, history, and purpose. It's comforting to know the test you're taking doesn't have glaring flaws.

"The Buros Center for Testing has two divisions, one that focuses on commercially-available tests (BIMM) and one that focuses on non-commercially available tests (BIACO)," says Chad Buckendahl, director of the Buros Institute for Assessment Consultation and Outreach, University of Nebraska-Lincoln.

According to the Buros Website: "Buros does not develop or recommend tests, but operates in similar fashion to *Consumer Reports* as an independent source for users or potential users of tests and testing programs. We evaluate these tests against the Standards for Educational and Psychological Testing (American Educational Research Association, American Psychological Association, and National Council on Measurement in Education, 1999)." These are the guidelines that the professional testing community uses to develop and evaluate the validity of their programs.

"With respect to corporate tests, I am assuming that you are talking about instruments that are used as part of the employment or promotion process," Chad Buckendahl explains. "These types of tests will sometimes be cognitive (e.g., intelligence), affective (e.g., personality), or a combination of these." Organizations will use these differently depending on their specific use. "The important thing for a testing organization would be to collect and document validity evidence that supports the use of the scores for the intended purposes."

Thinking From the Past

"As a general recommendation (not a Buros recommendation, a 'Chad' recommendation) for preparing for these types of tests, it is important to know how the instruments were developed. If the instrument was developed on successful people in the respective company, then doing your homework and finding out what makes them successful would be one strategy," Chad Buckendahl says. "However, in terms of actually taking these tests, it is important to answer the affective questions very honestly (not trying to guess the 'right' answer) because *there may be validity checks built into the instrument to determine whether the candidate is consistent with his or her responses versus what one might expect with similar responses or profiles.*" There are many of these instruments and uses out there.

Sometimes flawed assessments are administered. Think along the 1960s style of psychotherapist Rollo May, when there were no computers and instant communication. If you continuously seek identity, you may end up asking whether you have any significance at work. But reasoning four decades later in this digital age, even if you know who you are, do you wonder why insight about you is so important to the corporation's databases?

Will your organization eventually sell those databases to marketing firms? Will an employee take home a laptop and perchance lose your "private" personality profile?

Rollo May might have asked you, "How many more years can you stand your own powerlessness at work?" And today, the studies of workers on their jobs who complain they feel sick from the pollution in the office building air may really feel sick from powerless, stress, and lack of control over job issues.

Measuring Control at Work

Calmness on the job is healthy. According to the March 23, 2006, BBC News (*news.bbc.co.uk/1/hi/uk/4832744.stm*), a British study and survey of 4,000 civil servants in London office buildings by Dr. Mai Stafford and colleagues at the Epidemiology and Public Health department of University College, London Medical School, noted that workers reporting that they didn't have support from co-workers and control over the environment by being able to open windows or turn down heating felt the worst.

The more control people had over their jobs, the healthier they stated themselves to be. The study found that "sick building syndrome" had less to do with an unhealthy workplace environment and more to do with job stress.

Even though work environments such as air pollution in offices and factories, overheating, or cold exist and are very important to employee health, some 14 percent of men and 19 percent of women in the survey reported five or more symptoms associated with the "sick building" syndrome.

The quality of the buildings studied appeared too good to have had such bad effects on health. Stressful social and psychological issues made an impact on the workers' health. The more control you have over the social and environmental factors of your job, the healthier you feel.

That's why if you're designing tests, surveys, questionnaires, or other assessments, you might want to contact clients looking to study how much control workers have over the details of their daily work life. There's opportunity in the marketplace to design all types of assessments at varying levels and to advise individuals or businesses on how to take these types of tests.

Do the corporate test instruments tell you how to change your attitude or your job description?" Do you find that even as an executive you have little or no significance at work because you are not allowed to influence others?

Rollo May might have surmised that the next step could be apathy, but today your organization solves problems and achieves results through corporate assessments, team-building, and leadership training.

You can use Anne's creativity test for writers, which you'll find in full in Appendix A, as a template. Be sure to create the same number of questions for each category. Some tests are flawed because certain categories are more popular choices, and the test designer develops more questions for the popular categories. For the 35 questions in Anne's assessment, there are seven questions for each category of the following five opposing (contrasting) personality traits:

➤ Grounded/Verve.

➤ Rational/Enthusiastic.

➤ Decisive/Investigative.

➤ Loner/Outgoing.

➤ Traditional/Change-Driven.

Another test that uses these same pairs is Anne's Job Task Interest Classifier, which you'll find in Appendix B. This test is designed to measure your preferred style of writing and relationships at work. Scores are used to match your personality preferences with the preferences of potential employers and/or teammates, or for team-building exercises.

What Results Employers Want to See on a Personality Test

When employers consider your confidential personality test result, they are looking for your ability to connect with others and communicate clearly. Being misunderstood is one of the main reasons for conflict in the workplace.

Certain types of job descriptions don't want a creative, artistic, bubbly personality in jobs that require adaptability to routine, accuracy, and speed. Other job descriptions want creativity within a set of company rules coupled with the ability to persuade, sell, motivate, inspire, and train co-workers, and attract customers while focusing on amplifying the company's image, purpose and growth goals.

Connecting with co-workers and managers is the secondary reason you're hired or promoted. The hidden primary reason you're hired or promoted is a financial one: You pose the least financial risk, whether it be in insurance, accommodation, or simply taking a chance on your potential based on credentials, experience, and certification.

? ? ? ? ? ? ? ?

Chapter 2

Types of Tests
Given

Reviews give you a wider horizon of perspective in order to make choices. In addition to the online reviews, Annie Murphy Paul's 2004 book, *The Cult of Personality*, notes that your local university or public library usually has "a set of Mental Measurements Yearbooks" containing "basic information" about various "personality tests" or abilities assessments. Read psychologists' critiques of these assessments.

Your goal is to understand that workplace decisions may be made about you by your employer based on abilities tests or personality assessments that may or may not be valid. Always ask for feedback on any assessments you take, and ask your employer to keep your results confidential.

Personality or abilities tests need to be handled as confidential medical records. Find out whether or not test results are given to your health insurance company along with medical information. Psychological testing should be confidential and not stored in open-ended databases in your employer's human resources department.

Users of psychological tests include employers, teachers, school guidance and career counselors, outsourced consultants, clergy, and workshop leaders who are independent contractors. Is the person administering the tests trained in the pitfalls to avoid hindsight? Has your boss researched alternative types of assessments and given you a choice as to which you prefer?

What decisions are being made about you based on taking corporate tests? Are assessments part of the hiring process, or given mainly to executives to build better teams?

The Number of Tests

You're going to do better on tests some days and worse on other days. According to Michael R. Abramowitz's article, "Cultivate Your Job Personality One Test At A Time: Fight Layoff Blues By Discovering What Career Suits You Best" in the *Palm Beach Post* (online at *www.palmbeachclassifieds.com/employment/jobs/main/jobs_personality_main.html*) regarding personality profiles, "...the results often are hit-and-miss, and unexpected challenges can arise." The question you may be asking is: How many tests does it take to hire you?

Is your employer really going to rely on only one corporate test to hire you? That depends upon the test. If you're taking one test that screens out angry, disgruntled, even potentially violent people, perhaps one test is enough.

When it comes to job skills, abilities, or performance, how many tests are enough? A job-skills and abilities test might be sufficient, depending upon the particular job. It costs anywhere from nothing at a continuing education career center to about one thousand dollars with a private testing company to take assessments.

Tests really measure insight. To take corporate tests, you need to learn how to interpret those tests.

Testing is a tool for improving individual effectiveness at work by building better teams. Corporate testing of skills, accuracy, speed, and honesty usually is offered in the recruiting office when you first apply for a job.

"Executives like to have a system," Anne was told recently by a testing professional. "That's why most corporations do testing. They give personality assessments to their employees for the purpose of *team-building*." There's one system for hiring and another for team-building. Managers think that if you ask an employee a question, you can hope that an individual will tell you the truth.

What's Your Employer's Attitude Regarding Corporate Test Results?

Brian Jones of San Diego, California, who offers "Online Career and Personality Assessments Using the Myers-Briggs Type Indicator (MBTI), 16PF, Strong Interest Inventory, FIRO-B, and TKI, " says, "Most of my clients use the MBTI ® for team building, coaching, or executive development. Some want to use it for recruiting, but it's not designed for that purpose. It doesn't measure skills, abilities, or predict behavior."

When you "test" personality, it's an assessment, not a test. It can be a classifier, questionnaire, or indicator. That's one reason why the company where you work may request that you take a personality profiling assessment.

Your first step in taking corporate tests is to find out your employer's attitude toward corporate test results. Then find out what trait each answer signifies and how the test is scored and interpreted.

There are wide varieties of corporate tests, and there are published learning/training materials and brief workshops on how to administer these tests, usually given as extended studies courses on various campuses or by trainers who give these tests in corporations.

Corporations realize that people on teams differ, and little if anything will change them. Corporate tests analyze what temperament professional Dr. David Keirsey calls "different drummers."

Corporate Testing Is About Identity Seeking

The corporate world currently deals with "disengaged identity." The potential in disengaged job-related personality identity is perhaps a bit similar to the disengaged sexuality described by psychoanalyst Rollo May in the late 1960s in his book, *Love and Will*.

Do corporations hungry for identity pore over corporate tests to measure their position relative to the competition? Is the corporate test seen as an extension of a company's identity?

Employees at all levels are supposed to present a specific "corporate" image of their employers to the world. When hired, most are briefed on the philosophy or mission of the company, which usually is formed from the employer's identity, personality, and attitudes.

A corporation carries the identity of its most powerful manager, and it wants its employees (and teams) to have a similar identity.

Employers hire people smarter than the boss to solve problems. You're hired because you connect well with others not because you're well-connected. Certain corporate tests show how well you fit in with the group.

Who Can Access, Administer, and Score Corporate Tests?

Most people are surprised to learn that corporate tests aren't always designed, offered, and scored by degreed and credentialed psychologists. Often testing falls to the HR department. And individuals with degrees in human resource management are likely assigned the task of giving you these assessments in your workplace. Increasingly, independent test administrators are contracted. They visit corporations to test your teams or groups.

Almost anyone with a four-year college degree can take a short course in how to administer a variety of corporate tests. You fill out a form noting that you're qualified, usually by a specially approved course that you took through extended studies on a campus or by private firms preparing you to administer a certain corporate test.

You don't need a doctorate in psychology to give a wide variety of corporate tests to teams in a corporate setting. Test publishers make money by selling the tests to corporations and to outside fee-for-service independent contractors who have clients—corporations—where they visit to talk to teams on team building, give the assessments, and discuss their interpretation after the tests are scored. Usually the tests are sent away to be scored at the test publisher's scoring center.

You can become certified and qualified to purchase the assessment, learn to score it or have it scored, and administer the indicator to others. With or without a degree, you can buy books on how to interpret various corporate tests. Or you can contact the training departments of the many test publishers.

Books on taking corporate assessments currently available include:

➤ *How to Master Psychometric Tests* by Mark Parkinson.

➤ *Ace the Corporate Personality Test* by Edward Hoffman.

➤ *Interpreting Personality Test: A Clinical Manual for the MMPI-2, MCMI-III, CPI-R, and 16PF* by Robert J. Craig.

For an opposing view, read *The Cult of Personality: How Personality Tests Are Leading Us to Miseducate Our Children, Mismanage Our Companies, and Misunderstand Ourselves* by Annie Murphy Paul.

Identity

Corporate testing materials usually are sent to those administering the tests and to people interested in learning to score or interpret the scores. Before you take any corporate tests, jot down answers to the following questions by looking at the interpreting and scoring materials disseminated by corporate assessment/test publishing companies. Get to know yourself, your personality identity, by making a list in a journal.

There are no "right" or "wrong" answers on a corporate assessment of personality or decision-making preferences. You don't study for corporate testing unless you're being tested for skills, such as computer keyboarding accuracy and speed or knowledge of technology. Instead, executives being tested on team-building skills and personality traits prepare to take corporate tests by making lists of their own personality preferences using the process of journaling.

Your Corporate Test Preparation Journal

1. List five reasons why you and people on your team say that they don't like the decisions made on their jobs. What do you like about your career? What do you like and dislike about the decisions of people on your team?

2. List five leadership traits. Which traits do you have? Is it more comfortable for you to lead or follow?

3. Ask in advance which tests are given at work. Learn to analyze, interpret, and score those assessments.

4. Purchase a copy of the test from the publisher, a testing center, or continuing education/career counseling office. Take the tests privately.

5. Discern between competency and training.

6. Research how your employer applies test results to your job.

7. List the methods you use to solve problems at work.

8. Compare your boss's attitude with your team's attitude toward test results.

9. Journal some traits regarding your personality identity. Is your job identity multidimensional? Or does one word describe your job identity?

10. List any health problems that have been created by job stress.

Assessing Employees

What honest answers are best for your career? And who uses corporate testing for which purposes? So if much of corporate testing doesn't predict behavior, why is it given? Why do so many Fortune 500 companies use corporate testing, and especially the MBTI?

Companies such as Merck, Sheraton, Kaiser Permanente, Pepsi, and Clorox, and many more, have administered corporate tests to employees. Check out the huge list of major corporations using certain assessments on the link from Brian Jones's Website (*www.DiscoverYourPersonality.com*). Jones also publishes an informational online newsletter detailing a variety of corporate assessments.

Answering the Tests

You may choose to take career, entrepreneur, interpersonal relations, and/ or leadership tests, or take an entire test package for greatest benefit. Entire groups are frequently tested. If you are to be true to yourself, how will the resulting answers influence your job or career?

Corporate testing shows you how you make decisions, take in information, and process facts. Your identity is led out of its hiding place. Testing reveals how you influence those around you, and how others influence you at work. You're tested because your corporation wants you to get along with the rest of your team's unchanging differences. Your corporation has a good reason to test you: Its production and profit depends on the team functioning smoothly as a unit in spite of the differences pulling in all directions.

Fitting Into the Group

Tests are not about how others see you as much as they are about how you see yourself.

Getting fired a generation ago "for not fitting into the group" used to be written on pink slips kept in hidden files, and sometimes written in coded letters. Currently, when a new employer calls for references, the individual is told that only dates of employment may be given out. Otherwise, it opens a door for a former employee to sue an employer for defamation of character. Ask any human resource managers, "How many people are let go because of answers on corporate tests designed to improve team-building skills?" "None, of course," most will say in an interview.

Today if you're terminated it's so you can "move on to customized opportunities." You might still be told you're terminated now for "not connecting." Corporations like to think of teams as a family. There are even tests to screen employees for the potential to be disruptive, because employers are worried about too much anger in the workplace.

You can select any answer on a corporate test as long as it's honest. The question remains whether under stress at work you see yourself the way you'd like to be or the way others see you.

Team-Building Tests

You take team-building tests so that your employer can learn how to capitalize on the differences between team members. What you, your team members, and boss learn from taking corporate tests is how to observe *clues* to each individual's natural talents. Then this information can be used to position each person.

In a corporate world where nearly everyone is reading how to position him- or herself first, reality dictates that personality "clues" be organized to position each employee where individual talents are transformed into strengths for the company. The reasoning is that any strength for the company also will manifest strength for the individual.

It's assumed that a person's health will benefit by being in a job where the particular talent is used joyfully. The "radical thinking builds great teams" emphasis is practiced by some executive coaches. References to Marcus Buckingham and Donald O. Clifton's book, *Now, Discover Your Strengths*, often are cited by executive and leadership coaches.

Deep Trust Is Needed Among Team Members

The radical thinking is simply that you build a team based on "complementary strengths," as cited in *Now, Discover Your Strengths*. The book reports that before you can build any team based on people *complementing* one another, deep trust among the team members is required.

Without total trust, there's no way to express the different points of view without the different views being interpreted as conflict. You can't build a team when each member pulls in a different direction. "My way or the highway" is one outcome of conflicting views on any team matter, however trivial.

Deep trust also is needed between husband and wife, and between parents and children. These also are teams. Teams are partners. Interestingly, in life or on a team, the concept of complementing one another is a priority ahead of complimenting one another.

A Corporation Seeks Insight Into How You See Yourself

According to the Australian firm Optimum Corporate Services, its profile analysis, called Profile Plus, is an assessment that provides "individually analyzed insight" into how you see yourself. A corporation also is seeking insight when you answer a questionnaire that will profile and score you on your decision-making skills or how you see yourself. Optimum also offers its Decision-Making Test.

What a corporation really wants is an understanding of your logic and reasoning skills. The bottom line is that you have to make good decisions. A good decision solves problems, is cost-effective, gets results others easily can follow, and increases production, revenue, and retention.

Executives Require Systems

Corporate tests are based on systems in use by executives. In corporations, nearly every decision is made according to a system. It follows that assessments are administered according to a rational system based on decision-making.

At the executive level, time used for decision-making is rapidly decreasing. Teams now are required to make decisions formerly made by one manager. And members of teams may not agree or get along due to different levels of experience or variations of personalities, attitudes, or aptitudes.

You Take a Corporate Test to Reduce Risk

You are hired because you pose the least amount of risk to your boss. Your employer's final goal is risk reduction, which helps determine bottom-line profit. Corporate tests are there to make sure you pose the least financial risk. Corporate testing for your employer is called a "strategic initiative." The assessment isn't "given"; it is "deployed." Corporations use words that come straight from the military service, banking, and government. A corporate test reassures the employer that you already operate at work in a more "timely and fiscally sound manner."

Do You Have Time to Make Rational Decisions?

You prepare to take a corporate test by emphasizing how you can best build teams and reduce risk in order to improve your company's profit bottom line. How well you perform on corporate tests may depend upon how rational your decisions are under less time available. But with teams making the same decision, there is less responsibility allotted to one person's input.

There are time constraints on how long you have to make good decisions. Because, as an employee, executive, or manager of any given corporation, you'll be evaluating or hiring, how does your manager further up know whether you will consider in the short time allowed all the information put before you? What important facts will you skip in order to make a decision by a deadline?

With a team, you hope that someone will pick up a detail you overlooked. You're given less time to do your required work and at the same time you're distracted by a need to control your team. It's a juggling act called multitasking in the face of having to make decisions. In fact your organization makes hundreds of decisions each day—shared among many people who may or may not get along.

How Fast Do You Make Good Decisions?

In come the decision-making assessments to help the employer choose the right people. To function well in your job (or be promoted to management) you have to make good decisions quickly and instinctively. The assessment measures the proportion of good decisions you make. The benefit of taking a decision-making test is to your corporation. It's a big-picture outcome pointing to improving your employer's bottom-line profit.

The more *good* decisions you make, the more you improve the profit of the company where you're employed. That's why you may be given the OCS Decision-Making Test. Testing is good both for you and for your company.

You take the test with OCS's Decision-Making Test results as your goal; "to be selected or to select staff based on making rational decisions and solving problems" by what OCS notes on its Website as "anticipating future implications, encouraging participation from others in their team, handling issues objectively but with empathy, implementing decisions with assurance and strategic planning, and assessing outcomes."

Critics of Corporate Testing

There are those who oppose corporate testing. Many corporations don't take sides when corporate testing is the norm. The rationale of corporate testing has been challenged in books such as Annie Murphy Paul's 2004 book, *The Cult of Personality*. Most corporate tests are based on Carl Jung's writings on personality types. Corporate tests today are respected by many organizational psychologists and human resource managers, and not by the academic psychology profession.

In some studies, 47 percent of people tested fell into the same category on a second administration of the MBTI. (This was noted by Barbara Ehrenberg in her 2005 book, *Bait and Switch*, in the section on corporate testing. She took most of these tests while applying for corporate jobs as part of her research for writing the book.)

Can You Prepare for Corporate Tests?

You can learn to interpret the various corporate tests before you take them by understanding which answers signify what score (or answers) your job requires. But is this honest? And what happens if you are put in a role that's making you sick? If you are true to yourself, but what you are is not what the company needs, what will happen to your job? Will you be terminated? Or will your job description change?

Find out how seriously your employer takes corporate assessments and whether the scoring or interpretation is accurate. If some of these tests are only 47 percent accurate most of the time, would your team-building skills depend on the tests or on hands-on training in team-building?

Corporations are built of digitized utilitarian beings employed for their adaptability, commitment, and reliability. What corporations fear most from employees is risk. That's why corporations test teams.

If the corporate testing is done solely to help with team-building, to help people cooperate instead of compete, perhaps the focus should be on the company competing against an outside force rather than looking inward toward the members of its teams that pull in opposite directions because of personality dissonance. On the other hand, the company is made up of people with different and conflicting dimensions of personality. Team-building conflicts are a company's enemy within.

With practice, you can adapt more quickly to change, to alter your behavior in the moment in order to operate on an unstable team. Your first step is to learn to take corporate tests by interpreting them and anticipating the answers.

Most anyone can become an expert in interpreting or training to administer the tests in a brief workshop. But can you actually *study* for it? Only if you know beforehand what the answers signify—what rational decisions are like (weighing pros against cons on a list) compared to choices based on emotions.

Ask the person giving corporate tests what method the company expects you to use in order to make decisions under stress in your role. In a timed test of decision-making ability, will you be measured based upon how many vital details you did not overlook?

One way to prepare to take corporate tests is to read books on how to understand them. If you're taking the 16PF or some of the other personality assessments, you might want to read Robert J. Craig's *Interpreting Personality Tests: A Clinical Manual for the MMPI-2, MCMI-III, CPI-R, and 16PF.*

Some personality assessments help people better understand why conflicts may develop. Your boss wants to know how you control your own needs, such as your need for recognition or privacy when interacting with others at work. Several corporate tests measure how you behave toward another person, and tests are on the market that show how you would like others to behave. Some of these tests are classified under the category of tests of emotional maturity. Not all corporations test for emotional maturity. Most test only for job skills and abilities.

Corporate testing is about obtaining insight, hindsight, and foresight regarding employees at various levels and their teams. What test-takers want to know is how to avoid the pitfalls. Obtaining critical insights into your need for *inclusion, control,* and *affection* through corporate testing may accompany a workplace seminar on managing conflict.

? ? ? ? ? ? ? ?

Chapter 3

Conquering the Fear of
Corporate Testing

The biggest fear corporate test-takers have is repercussions. People on a team fear the consequences of revealing and recording their own point of view if they don't trust the team members.

Workplace assessments look at personality traits, honesty/integrity values, decision-making abilities, teamwork, critical thinking strategies, cognitive abilities, and job skills performance. Tests also can measure self-insight.

To prepare for a personality test, you need to make a list of self-discovery questions and practice answering them. You can answer a variety of self-discovery questions and take short personality tests online (free) for practice. One is Color Quiz (*www.colorquiz.com/*), a free, five-minute personality test based on decades of research by color psychologists around the world, according to the Website. Another is Similar Minds.com (*www.similarminds.com*), which offers a variety of 16 Type Jungian tests, the Big Five tests, Personality Disorder Test, Intelligence Test, Eysenck Personality Test, and other assessments.

There also are links to a Ph.D.–certified personality test at Tickle.com (*www.tickle.com*), as well as to a career personality profile at FunEducation (*www.funeducation.com/PersonalityProfile/*). After playing around with tests of personality, you will be able to make up your own questions that lead to self-discovery.

What the tests may not tell you is what employers are looking for: positive thinking. If you describe yourself optimistically, you can point out areas of self-insight. No one wants to hire someone with negative thoughts about his or her potential, persistence, or self-insight.

To describe characteristics that may be perceived as negative in a positive light, tell your interviewers three ways how you will affect the company's bottom line. Make a list of exactly how you will do so, and then choose the top three. For example:

1. You pose the least financial risk because _____. (Fill in one main fact, such as your good health and energy, willingness to work for a certain wage, and volunteer work that presented an excellent image of that company.)

2. You charismatically attract customers by giving presentations based on fact-filled, exciting, enthusiastic public speaking.

3. You're willing to talk to customers to explain benefits and advantages of product backed up by explaining briefly in plain language scientific studies of the product backed up by your aptitude for organizing events, data, and/or people.

If you have had no job experience, simply state that you have no previous deleterious experience to unlearn and lots of opportunities to turn challenges into building blocks. If you've had many negative experiences, just tell your interviewers that challenges open doors of opportunity. Crises give you the tools that allow you to learn from challenges.

Those tools—called hindsight, insight, and foresight—help you avoid pitfalls and blind spots. If you've had negative experiences or long-term job-free gaps, report that crises are visionary learning environments that offer alternative routes to navigate.

Negative experiences are motivational tools to help you to think outside the box. With creativity, charisma, inspiration, or versatility, you can describe your potentially negative attributes in a positve light by displaying that you are an enigmatic person whose goal is for the public good—*pro bono publico*—and that your objective is utility.

Tell your interviewers that the employer's benefit in hiring you is that you pose the least financial risk to the company. As an enthusiastic, charismatic person you are excellent at maintaining connections with your team of peers. Your value lies in the use you make of each day. And emphasize that your work ethic will create a great image for the company.

Think of the best possible day that might be possible in a workplace environment. Then describe yourself in positive terms. Put yourself in your employer's shoes. Whatever your answers are, ask yourself: Would I hire someone like me? If you stay on the positive track with your self-insight, you'll avoid most of the pitfalls of personality testing.

Be receptive to the questions without resisting them. You're not an attorney in a courtroom setting arguing with the judge when you visualize personality assessment questions. Instead of analyzing the questionnaire, just answer positively exactly what the question asks you.

You've heard many times that the first spontaneous answer usually is the right answer. This works on most types of tests, including personality assessments. Answer the questions as best you can with the aim of fitting into the group or looking at the answer strictly from the employer's point of view.

An excellent book on what an employer looks for in an employee regarding personality preferences is found in the book *The Organization Man* by William Whyte. Another good reference that mentions Whyte's book (as a tip for taking personality assessments) is Mark Parkinson's book *How to Master Personality Questionnaires*.

What Employers Want to See on Personality Tests

What personality tests are revealing to employers is what they want: an extroverted, conservative man who is competitive and not full of anxiety tremors. The personality test is supposed to show employers what a "well-adjusted" man "looks like" on an assessment.

The problem with *The Organization Man*'s ideal corporate male is that it didn't study women or much diversity in personality. It leaves out the entrepreneurial man who fears his father or has authority problems, is introverted, and had problems deferring to his father.

Before you take a personality test, find out the specific job requirements and the character of the corporation. Employers only want to see positive answers. You're usually told when asked "what are your weaknesses" to say marvelously, "working too many hours because I enjoy this type of work."

The trait employers want to see on personality tests is how positive you are. If you're going to take a personality profile, give the company and its leaders the same scrutiny. Find out through the job description whether the company is similar to your personality. If you are traditional and conservative and the company is traditional and conservative, it could be a match. If the company is visionary and poised for constant change, and you need to use your imagination and are willing to adapt with the shifting, then it also could be a match. Staying positive relies on working with people similar to yourself in values, talents, and traits.

Why Employers Fear the Entrepreneur Personality

Many executives and job applicants are concerned that employers don't want to hire people who score high on aptitude for being an entrepreneur—unless you're hired as an independent contractor. In a sense, that's true.

In 1956, when Simon & Schuster first published *The Organization Man* by William H. Whyte, executives discussed stirring observations about the relationship between a man and his father, and a boss and a male employees.

The book focused on males employed by corporations, and observations ensued regarding why the book recommended job applicants taking corporate personality tests practice silently repeating statements such as "I loved my father and my mother, but my father a little bit more."

What employers were seeking to recruit, according to *The Organization Man*, published again in 2002 by the University of Pennsylvania Press, focused on a stylized, conservative man who won't rock the boat. Corporations wanted men who liked the way the corporate leaders ran everything.

The book instructed men to present a positive personality image of a guy who "doesn't worry much, doesn't care for books or music, loves wife and children, but will never let them get in the way of his work (for the corporation)." These items from *The Organization Man* also appear in Mark Parkinson's book, *How to Master Personality Questionnaires*. Employers are still looking for this type of conservative, extroverted employee—male or female—who doesn't worry much and won't make waves.

What Employers Think of Entrepreneurs

You can learn a lot about whether your personality matches the character of a firm by reading that corporation's annual report. Entrepreneurs are perceived and received differently from other job applicants in many HR departments that do extensive personality and abilities testing.

Successful independent contractors negotiate business-to-business deals with corporations or government. They don't ask for employment. Business failures line up asking for a job. So runs the assumption.

Employers may associate sudden career change with sudden personality change. Both may be viewed by the corporate world as forms of "snapping."

Unless an employer advertises for independent contractors, online part-time facilitators/teachers, adjunct professionals, or entrepreneurs, saying timorously that you ran your own business for years could be a mistake.

The employer may think you didn't earn enough and had to close your business. You failed. Now you're welcome to the world of outsourcing—when an employer wants you to work without health insurance, paid vacations, and pension benefits. Saying you offered outsourced services to your employer reflects an attitude of laconic but steadfast loyalty.

Here's why part-time or former entrepreneurs applying for full-time employment often are rejected when they apply for staff jobs: Employers are still worried that entrepreneurs are afraid of male authority figures.

Employers think entrepreneurs are risk-takers and will hire them when they need a high risk-taker, usually for temporary work. Historically, the entrepreneur has been psychoanalyzed, and the results have been passed from one employer to another since the 1960s.

Back in 1964, the September 19th issue of *Business Week* ran an article titled "Psychoanalyzing the Small Businessman." *Business Week* based the piece on a1964 Cornell University study of the personality traits of entrepreneurs (which didn't include women).

In 1990 Anne wrote an article discussing the 1964 Cornell study, titled "Entrepreneurs, Unlimited...A good Alibi Not to Go to Work Could Spell Success," which appeared in her "On-The-Job" column in the February 25–March 3, 1990 issue of *Professional Opportunity Magazine*. The column urged readers to look again at the original 1964 Cornell University study and include women.

The 1964 Cornell study of the male entrepreneur concluded that a guy opens his own business to become like the father figure he has replaced (because the father figure wants exclusive possession of power). Scholars reported that the entrepreneur is elite, that no average man can create a business: "It's truly an act of the highest order requiring motivation bordering on obsession."

Executives thought entrepreneurs feared male authority figures. Corporate leaders interpreted the1964 study as suggesting male entrepreneurs competed with a "weak" father that the sons didn't want to emulate.

Scholars noted that entrepreneurs hate routine, are fleeing poverty, and are "early starters." According to the *Business Week* article, as a male entrepreneur, your strongest drive will be "to escape the intolerable immediate by initiating a line of action leading to an unknown magical future."

Employers still feel that independent contractors and other entrepreneurs, including fee-for-service telecommuters, may feel that working for someone else is the most insecure job in the world. But once on their own, having to please the customer and keep revising services until the customer's requirements are met, means hustling daily without praise, fringe benefits, or vacations.

Executives who read that entrepreneurs open their firms because they are afraid of a hostile father and victimized mother are reluctant to hire independent contractors as employees if their businesses fail. Individuals taking a personality test are expected to show loyalty to the corporation and a positive attitude.

What to Do and Say Before the Interviews

Conservative, traditional corporations may be afraid to hire you if you reveal in a personality test by scoring high on visionary, forward-looking, change-oriented, non-traditional workplace or lifestyle choices that you strongly follow the Thoreau personality preference, which describes individuals who want to "Go confidently in the direction of your dreams. Live the life you've imagined."

If you check boxes that show a preference for abstract, visionary, and change-oriented (non-traditional) preferences, the conservative corporations might think you are not going to follow the rules of successful giant corporations that followed tradition and that believe if it is not broken, don't fix it. If you believe in breaking the product or its rules and building something new to improve it, that's visionary, forward-thinking that is change oriented.

You need to match your preferences to the mission of the company. It has been said that the mission or philosophy of a corporation matches the personality of its founders or current CEO. In other words, corporations have characters just as people have personalities. To read more about the character of corporations, see Rob Goffee and Lehman B. Fletcher's book, *The Character of a Corporation: How Your Company's Culture Can Make or Break Your Business*. According to the editorial review of this book, "Corporate culture is more than just a way to set the tone at work—it also affects the bottom line."

If your dreams are change-oriented and visionary, you're not going to follow those tradition-oriented successful giant corporations of the past or look at historic polls, or perhaps read traditional magazines such as the pre-1960s type of family and history-centered articles that appeared in the *Saturday Evening Post*. Lots of businesses today look to tradition, family, and what worked historically, to develop products. In contrast, visionary businesses look to the future of technology, such as putting easier-to-operate, less costly, and smaller digital computers, appliances, cameras, Internet cell phones, electronic life-saving systems or other mobile playing and recording, or diagnostic devices into the hands of students, parents, physicians, and seniors living alone.

If your personality preferences motivate you to select the box on a personality test that asks if you'd prefer rapid change-oriented and visionary work environments, you're probably going to read future-oriented publications and inquire how a business might be improved by change, rather than by looking backwards to successful tradition that in the past worked well and still may not be broken or need fixing in the traditional sense. For example, a personality assessment question might ask you whether you would rather work for a company that claims to run the tightest ship in the shipping business or a corporation that is looking into putting satellite Internet-related devices into space, cameras, and phones, or testing new ways to use gene therapy?

Another test-question choice might ask you whether you'd prefer to work for a company based on taking public polls or looking into historically what worked well in the past for a particular product. Would you rather work for a company selling tangible appliances such as vacuum cleaners, irons, refrigerators, or cars? Or would you prefer to work for a company selling ideas such as think tanks, advertising agencies, trends-reporting firms, and marketing communications research companies? Would you prefer to work for a company selling abstract ideas or practical advice based on factual research and statistics? Before you interview with any company, make a list of what the company represents in its mission and goals. Is it abstract or concrete in its philosophy?

That's why before your interviews it's smart to use clues from job descriptions and read company histories from corporate publications before taking a personality assessment. Ask for a company report and a practice test.

Look at the four or five possible choices. On the practice test make a list of the choices and put the abstract choices in one column and the concrete choices in another column. Put the change-oriented, futuristic, visionary choices in one column and the tradition-based choices that follow successful giant corporations in another column.

Now you can analyze your choices in plain view. You're going to choose either the abstract ideas or the practical, logistical skills that you'd want to use on a job. You'll be able to select whether you want a job with a corporation that emphasizes the success of tradition or the visionary, change-oriented aspect of looking into the future. Which choice makes you feel more at ease? Once you've made your choices, you'll get an idea of what the company's mission, philosophy, goal, and personality preferences of the people who run the corporation. By taking a practice test apart and viewing what choices you're given on an assessment, you'll be able to see whether the company has a character that is traditional or visionary.

Now you can match your own preferences with the company's character. By comparing opposite choices given to you on a personality assessment, you can see clues from the practice test of what the company is seeking from you.

If you're visionary and the company is traditional (and emphasizes benchmarking values that depend upon the "tight ship" rules and logistics of successful corporations of the past), then you can move on to another company more in line with your choices. IBM and Fed Ex have been used as examples of tradition-oriented companies in the past, and Microsoft in the past has been used as an example of a future-oriented, visionary company.

Before you set an interview appointment, obtain a practice test from the company or from the publisher of the assessment the company uses. Some sample tests may be in university libraries. Your best bet, if the company doesn't give out practice tests for you to peruse before an interview, would be to purchase the test a company uses from the publisher (if the publisher of the test will sell you a sample test). Or ask a school or private counselor, or an organizational psychologist to let you look at a sample test.

The research you're doing is part of your homework in finding out what the company considers to pose the least financial risk to it. Analyzing a test will help you get to know yourself better because you'll have more time to think about what answers represent the choices that really stand for your own values. Think of yourself in the job for 45 years. Would you be a good fit? Even though some people may change jobs every three or four years on average, there are still companies that employ people for many decades that are really a good fit in those jobs and are healthy in their work.

Here's how a sample list of choices would look. By looking at the possible choices on a sample test, it becomes easier to match your own values and preferences with the company's list of choices. Let's say the company wants a visionary, charismatic, enthusiastic executive with change-oriented, forward-looking ideas and practical applications of them. Here are possible choices.

At an office party you'd rather:

1. Talk to as many people as possible about your hobby.

2. Look for someone interested in talking about what worked well in the past that you wouldn't want to see altered. (An example would be a classic flavor of soda pop.)

3. Show pictures of your children to someone interested in child daycare at the office.

4. Ask someone how to create a video podcast about your new ideas for an invention.

5. Look for one person to talk to about your specific job description and its potential for promotion in the future.

6. You wouldn't go to office parties because you'd rather work online at home.

7. Ask whether anyone looks into the employee suggestion box and rewards good ideas.

8. Ask your boss if he or she would like to see your new invention or alteration of an existing gadget or company device that would save the company money.

9. Plan the office party yourself and invite a change-oriented speaker.

10. Do the catering for the office party and ask everyone how they liked your service and food.

Most personality assessments ask you to check boxes with your choices. Some decision-making tests could ask you to solve a problem by making a decision. Most of these answers are black or white. Either your choices show you're an extrovert or an introvert, that you're quiet or expressive. But you can choose boxes to check showing you're an expressive introvert or a closet (quiet) extrovert. Personality assessments differ in their questions based on the variety of publishers. Most test publishers don't like personality assessments to be called tests. They're assessments. Decision-making assessments are designed to help executives avoid the blind spots, the overlooked information.

Your career is subject to the pressures and stress of your job because more work is required in less time. Fifty years ago you would have had a lot more time to make a decision and a lot less information coming in for you to read. How will you decide what's important to consider before you decide? That's when a decision-making assessment comes in handy because your peers evaluate your assessment in many cases.

Scrutinize a sample test and look at the choices before you interview. Observe how the choices you list fall into opposite or contrasting categories based on your values and the company's values. The person in the company looking over your test results will most likely compare your answers with the vision and mission of the company, its character, and its values to see whether you match the job they have in mind. The decision is based on whether or not you pose the least financial risk to the company, how well you connect with your peers and employers, and how good an image you present of the company. As an employee, your image and the image you create represent the company's image.

Anything you write on your personality assessment could face you in an interview. The best answer to give in an interview reviewing your personality test results is that to prepare for the interview you did your homework in seeking direction from company information such as company publications and research.

Let the interviewer know that you've read the company's mission statement and goals, and that they are in line with your values and personality traits. Then be specific with concrete details about how your values will be of measurable cost-effective benefit to the company. Show results or explain how you would solve a particular problem. Companies hire you mainly for three reasons:

1. For your loyalty and ability to gain measurable results for the firm.

2. For your ability to solve specific problems in your field for the firm.

3. When you pose the least financial risk to the company and can connect well with its teams, peers, customers, suppliers, and corporate leaders.

At the interview, one example for an executive or new college graduate to give would be that you have recently taken courses in a foreign language representative of the country in which that corporation owns factories. Another would be that you have had an internship or experience purchasing imports related to what that company buys.

If you're an outsider, and the company won't give you any information, it's not a mark against you to ask for a sample assessment to peruse. Request the test by mail or phone unless you're writing a freelance article about the company as a corporate success story to submit on speculation to a magazine to which the company subscribes. Do library research on the company before calling.

Don't show up in person unless you're interviewing the boss for a freelance article to give free publicity to the firm, and you submit the article to a publication approved of by the company. If you're able to write a corporate success story case history about the firm and submit it to a publication, even if you're not paid, do so. Trade journals and employee newsletters (called house organs) often publish this material about employees and corporate leaders. Some publications do not pay the writer. But it will give you a chance to make yourself known.

At that time, it is acceptable to ask for a sample test. Don't make a pest of yourself. If the company denies a phone or mail request for a test to peruse, ask the name of the test. Then buy the test from the publisher or ask a licensed organizational psychologist or counselor to give you the test to look at and take home to analyze.

Look for clues in the choices. At any interview, find out the goals of the company. Don't ask for informational interviews, as few people have the time to spend with you, unless you're writing a corporate case history success story for a publication, paid or unpaid. The quickest way to get this type of interview is to ask a software manufacturer's public relations director if you can write a corporate case history success story about that company in which you want to interview for a job.

Usually, they'll give you the go-ahead and a press letter to interview the boss on how he or she likes their software or why that company switched to that software or other product. What the publicity director wants from the company is a one-and-a half page press release they can then put in a book and show to selected media about a corporation that switched to their software or other product.

Ask why they switched, get measurable results, and state how they solved a problem in the company that increased their revenue. When you've written your one-and-a-half-page press release/corporate success story case history, then ask for a job interview and to see a sample personality assessment that the corporation usually gives to job applicants.

If you're already an executive with that company, you may get a decision-making assessment instead of a personality test or both. If you are an executive already employed, you know the name of the test and the publishing company and can discuss with peers and coaches what traits are required to avoid blind spots in decision making as evaluated by peers and consultants or by organizational psychologists.

It's part of your homework to research the company so you can see whether your personality traits match the character of the corporation. Your personality style may be partly genetic, but the character of the corporation is set by who runs the company at a specific time in history. Leadership can change.

Most of your homework will be done before you first walk into the corporation for an interview. Tests and personality assessments usually are given before the employment interview. Anything you write on your personality test could face you in a later interview. The best answer to give in an interview reviewing your personality test results is that you're seeking direction and information from company publications. You may have several group and individual interviews before being hired or promoted.

Entrepreneurs create more than 400,000 businesses annually in the United States, and the media usually reports that more than 90 percent of new businesses fail in their first year. Employers often imagine the overwhelming scenario of all these entrepreneurs knocking on their doors for employment at varying levels of experience. Yet these frequently are the same people often contacted by business and government when outsourcing, contract work, and temporary services are needed.

Employers like to hire entrepreneurs as independent contractors, outsourced help, and in outside sales. If you're applying for a staff job after years of running your own show, you need to show an employer how you can solve specific problems in a corporation.

Keep your research narrow enough to find a problem in a particular department that you can solve. Use this information in your interview before you've taken your personality assessment. Take a personality test as if you were a career, executive, or life coach focused on positive thinking, loyalty, and optimism. On personality tests, joy of life becomes joy of work. Keep the answers positive, never bitter, and anxiety-free.

Always put yourself in your employer's frame of mind. Would you hire someone like you if you told the employer what you're thinking? It's a seller's market, unless you're the only one in town who knows how to do the job. A corporate test is supposed to convince your employer *why* you're the best person for the job. That's why coaches explore insight.

Life/Career Coaches

It should be noted that personality assessments alone should not be used to make a hiring decision. Michele Caron, life/career coach and creator of MyLifeCoach.com (*www.mylifecoach.com/*), Google's #1-ranked life-coaching site, works with her husband, Brian Pernick, who, she explains, "has a master's degree in teaching and a master's degree in education."

Clients for life and career coaches come from those seeking direction. Michele says:

> We are frequently contacted by those in the corporate world that are unsure of their career direction. Often, they have achieved a certain level of success, but are now confused about what comes next.
>
> Sometimes their managers recognize that the employee's performance, or fulfillment, is suffering, and they contact us for

assistance. For those unsure of career direction, we use the Myers-Briggs Type Indicator (MBTI) and Strong Interest Inventory.

Clients also seek understanding. They want to know how to interpret corporate testing and apply it to their specific situations. Clients want interaction with insight, rather than to simply view pages of career information.

"The MBTI and personality type theory help the client understand what they can excel at in a position, and what can bring them the most fulfillment," Caron says. "It can also help the client understand how they tend to interact with others at work, and how they can improve their own interpersonal skills." The MBTI is great for understanding the types of careers, or even the actual tasks in various careers, that make the best fit.

Clients want career advice organized in concrete steps. Canon says:

> The Strong Interest Inventory is great for a detailed breakdown of the specific career areas the client is most likely to enjoy. Even within the same company, clients, with the help of "the Strong," may realize that they would enjoy the marketing department much more than finance, for example. Again, like the MBTI, it can also help clients understand the specific task areas they are likely to excel at, such as understanding that they need to be creative, or they need to organize things, to get some personal satisfaction. We also help clients, departments and companies with teamwork and interpersonal relations.

The MBTI can be applied to a group, to find out how it is likely to behave as a team, and how each person likely fits into that team. As Canon explains:

> Teams that have very similar personality types tend to get along well, but they may come up with less creative answers to problems, or develop blind spots.
>
> Teams that have many different personality types may have more challenges interacting, and take more time to reach solutions, but their solutions tend to be better. The MBTI team analysis can help the similar teams learn to step outside of themselves sometimes, and help the dissimilar teams learn to get along and make everyone on the team feel valued and allow everyone to make a contribution.
>
> There is much more to the MBTI team analysis, and it can make a super team day exercise for a group in a corporate setting to build teamwork, communication and performance.

Corporate testing of leadership style and motivation helps clients see where they need to develop skills. "We also use the FIRO-B, typically for managers and executives," Caron says.

"It, especially when combined with the MBTI, can help clients understand their leadership style, how they can best motivate others, and where some areas for development may be, in order to get the most from themselves and those around them."

Caron says that "in all cases, the assessments are a starting point for further research, discussion, and understanding."

She explains how the client applies corporate test results:

> It may take some time and experience, once the client has the new knowledge provided by the assessments and discussion with the counselor or coach, before the client fully understands and can come to see how their personality type or interest areas fit into their work life (or personal life) and career direction.

Test result interpretations are referred to for a lifetime. "The assessments are a great investment for the client and their future," says Caron. "And when used properly, they can be referred back to over and over to help in self-development and making choices throughout the client's life."

Coaches frequently work with the two most popular assessments. "We think that everyone should do the MBTI and Strong Interest Inventory assessments at least once in his or her life (the earlier the better) to enable a lifetime of increased fulfillment, satisfaction, performance and happiness," Caron says emphatically.

Leadership Coaches Offer Corporate Tests

Testing chores may not always be assigned to a corporation's organizational psychologist. Instead the task may be given to a leadership and/or communications coach who also is an entrepreneur contracted by a corporation to solve problems through personality testing.

Leadership coaches usually have clients who are CEOs wanting to change the way they share information with or micromanage their employees. The coach may have an interdisciplinary background in public speaking, theater arts, sales, counseling, writing, training, communications, psychology, business management, theology, interviewing, or human resources.

You become a leadership and/or communications coach by attending a coaching school such as the Coaches Training Institute (CTI; *www.thecoaches.com/*). CTI offers training in coaching, leadership, and business development.

You can study to become a personal or life coach, executive or corporate coach, or coach-like manager or consultant, or take courses in corporate training and development. Often outsourced coaches are hired by a corporation's human resources department to administer a variety of corporate testing materials if the coach is trained and authorized to administer and interpret the assessment.

Scoring may be done through the mail by the test publisher's scoring headquarters, or the questionnaire may be self-scoring. Discussion emphasizes interpretation of the results.

How Corporate Testing Teaches Listening Skills

Corporate testing sets boundaries, holds you accountable to a personal development plan, and trains you to develop better listening skills. If your boss takes corporate tests along with the teams, the tools will reveal a boss's listening skills, measure how often an employer requests and respects ideas from workers, and show how much the boss values each employee's differences. Corporate testing, when interpreted in detail, opens doors to learning leadership skills.

When dealing with conflict on a team, coaches may (or may not) say that a male employee or boss might have trouble "accepting his feminine side within" because he's angry at his mother and sister. As a result of this repressed anger, fear, and insecurity, the stressed or depressed male manager could micromanage female peers through bullying.

Such bosses or co-workers throw childish tantrums to prove that they possess "manly" qualities. But such an out-of-control male boss or peer defines "manly" traits as achieving power through displaying anger and loud noise to maintain control. Female workplace bullies substitute the word *powerful* for *manly*. Both overcompensate.

Bosses and executives may not realize that masculinity, like femininity, is about responsibility, simplicity, and commitment in communication. With females at all levels of employment, corporate testing also separates the *demanding* boss or co-worker who makes time to listen to people, from the ruthless, abusive, and arrogant one who belittles you. (See Dan Vierria's article, "Devil Boss: Most of Us Know One—Or Are One," in the June 30, 2006, *Sacramento Bee*. It's about bully bosses, not corporate testing.) What corporate testing does encourage you to do is to get a handle on are your priorities. With managerial training supplemented by a system of corporate tests, you're staying on your toes and are accountable. You can develop your personality further.

What corporate personality testing doesn't do is give you a guide sheet for handing out consequences for overstepping boundaries to those at work that disparage, bully, or begrudge you. Some businesses use corporate testing and leadership training more than others. These include educational institutions as well as the largest Fortune 500 firms. Employers in certain medical and legal fields require you to have completed leadership training before you're hired.

How Do You See Yourself?

Most corporate tests are ideological. Some promote theories of employment. Others are accurate predictors of performance and job satisfaction. The tests mainly profile your personality and how you see yourself. Because the answers depend upon your response they are not about how your co-workers see you.

Is there a huge gap between how you see yourself—your insight into your own decisions and actions—and how others see you? Is there a gap between how your family sees you at home and how your co-workers see you at the office, and another gap between those opinions and how you see yourself? Are you afraid to admit to yourself what you really do or want to do under stress? What best-fit situation at work feels most comfortable for you when you have to make choices or process information?

Corporations Have Characters, Just as People Have Personalities

Just as people have personalities, so do corporations have characters—usually the character profile of the owner and/or founder. Companies are as tough to change as people. Companies have attitudes based on the attitudes of the most influential person running the organization. Job applicants are likely to see only the personality of the interviewer, which may or may not reflect the character of the corporation.

It's easy to discover a corporation's character. You ask the same questions as you'd ask when profiling an individual's personality: Where is the company going? What's the company's mission? Ask those in charge what the company is all about. What's its philosophy? Your personality profile is what you are about which represents your philosophy.

There's no test you can give a corporation, but if you ask what the company's mission is, those who run the organization will describe the firm as a benchmarking or visioning organization.

Benchmarking, according to The Benchmarking Exchange (TBE; *www.benchnet.com/wib.htm*), is defined as: "the process of identifying, understanding, and adapting outstanding practices from organizations anywhere in the world to help your organization improve its performance." A benchmarking corporation relies on tradition—using what's worked before compared to visionary companies that emphasize change and continuous looking for something different.

These two terms—*benchmarking* and *visioning*—come straight out of William Bridges, CCP's excellent book, *The Character of Organizations*, where they are fully described.

Tradition-seeking companies have different approaches to how to do business than forward-looking firms. The corporate world is divided between traditional corporations and change-oriented organizations. Traditional corporations are what Bridges calls "benchmarkers." And change-oriented firms are what Bridges calls "visionaries" or visioning companies.

The corporate world often uses the word *benchmarking*. The term has appeared in several books on organizational behavior to describe companies emulating what's worked well before. Tradition-seeking organizations model themselves after other companies that make or do something very successfully.

The traditional way that has worked well before becomes the standard way to determine how things ought to be made. "Benchmarkers," or, to use more familiar words, tradition-seeking companies, emulate the best, the most successful, and the most popular, according to Bridges. An example is the company that tries to model itself after Intel today or IBM (a decade before the compatibles competed). The tradition-seeking corporation simply wants to model itself after the most successful company where everything worked right.

Traditional corporation mottos emphasize not fixing what's not broken. You don't break something to improve it. You add on to what already works and has worked all along.

Companies possessing an "opposite" character or personality are called visionaries. Any company actually is reflecting the personality of its owner or founder. Visionary companies rely on introspection. They're idea-focused and change-seeking.

These companies have often been described as "visioning" new creations or inventions for the future or exploring hidden markets and applications.

Future-oriented companies enjoy new and better ways of doing what comes naturally—improving the quality and quantity of life. New ways of production must satisfy a great need.

Introspective, imaginative, visioning, or change-oriented companies seek new ways to think, however wild, imaginative, creative, and fantastic—as long as the applications run and the medicine cures.

The word *visioning* or *change-oriented* often is used in technology to describe a forward-looking, user-oriented, intuitive boss. Change-oriented employers hire the smartest people with the freshest ideas that can be turned into new products.

Change-oriented corporations are opposite in mission to traditional organizations. Change-oriented organizations include gene therapy research, cell phone manufacturers, and cutting-edge software firms.

Corporate Testing of Organizations Defines Communication Styles

Who is approachable at work? If you gave an organization a personality profiling assessment, you'd discover how a company's "character" defines how it communicates its needs. An organization shows you its particular gap that has to be bridged or filled.

When you take an individual corporate test, you show your employer how you communicate your needs at work and what deep well of sanity has to be filled by the daily details you shuffle. The character of your work defines how easily you communicate.

Visioning people feel energized when they are matched with visioning organizations. Benchmarking people have less wear and tear on their health when they work with benchmarking organizations. Before you take a corporate test, explore what styles of communication that organization uses: visionary or benchmarking.

? ? ? ? ? ? ? ?

Chapter 4

Preparing for Your Test

Time limits are your biggest enemy when taking corporate tests. Most of these assessments simply ask you to determine relationships. Instead of buying a ton of test guides filled with a few pages of general information you already know from high school and too many time-consuming practice activities, ask your company's HR department to give you the names of the tests you will take (and the publisher). Then research some reviews of those assessments online or in a public library.

You learn to take corporate tests by writing buzz words, which are positive image-arousing words. For example, "think of a pink elephant." Immediately, you visualize a pink elephant, and the image imprints on a pathway in your brain as a visual advertisement without actual graphic images. Other examples might be a shiny new car or a cold drink. The visualization in your mind will help you clearly understand the question, and formulate an answer

Generally corporate tests will measure abstract thinking, verbal fluency, numerical ability, perception, spatial reasoning, mechanical dexterity, or personality. Executives and managers may be given tests of decision-making or personality profiling.

Entry-level job applicants may have to take skills tests to see whether they perform to job specifications and requirements. Examples of skills tests would be performing at least 10,000 strokes on a ten-key adder, data entry accuracy and speed tests, keyboarding speed with accuracy, accounting ability, civil service exams, proficiency tests in your specialty, and tests of honesty (usually given to retail job applicants).

Corporate testing may also include a physical exam to make sure you're insurable and have no contagious diseases. Another test determines whether or not you are taking illegal drugs or abusing prescription medicines.

Different corporate tests are given to retail clerks, truck drivers, and teachers. You can prepare for corporate tests by purchasing a copy of the test from the publisher and practice taking the test. If you don't qualify to purchase the test (some publishers will not sell to individuals), then go to a career center of any adult education office or community college career counseling office and ask to take a series of tests. If you're not a student, you can pay a small fee charged to the public.

Tell the counselor or personnel assistant which tests you want to take. Then discuss the results with a counselor, who can interpret scores for you. There are plenty of books available on how to take personality tests, abilities tests, and psychometric tests. (See the Bibliography.)

The quickest way to prepare for a corporate test is to practice taking tests of reasoning ability and personality. (There are also test samples in this book.) Practice analyzing and answering the questions. Then design a few questions and answers of your own for practice in the same way as you take or design crossword puzzles for entertainment.

Focus on taking practice tests of *abstract thinking*. Corporate tests tend to emphasize abstract thinking skills, decision-making ability with evaluation of good or bad decisions, or personality profiles used for team-building. Find out what team, individual, or committee decides whether a decision is good or bad. How is the test scoring evaluated? Who interprets the score or outcome to you?

Take the various corporate tests online, such as the IQ tests, for their practice and rehearsal value. One example is the TOEFL Test (Test of English as a Foreign Language; available at *www.ets.org*). To find such tests, many of which are offered by consulting firms, search for "free corporate tests" in your favorite search engines. The more tests you take, the more familiar you become with how the test designers expect you to answer the questions.

What Values Does the Corporation Emphasize?

Prepare for corporate tests by researching what specific values a particular corporation represents. Then make a list of how closely a company's basic values match your own personality traits. On one side of a sheet of paper list any self-discovery questions and answers about your own personality preferences and abilities. On the other side of the paper, list the company's general values along with detailed requirements for the specific job.

On that list match your abilities to the specific job description of duties and tasks. After that's done, match your personality traits and values with the values, attitudes, and character of the company.

If the company's values are traditional and conservative and your general values are visionary, imaginative, and focused on rapid changes, it's not a match. If the job description says you must perform a routine task, such as repair computers or manage an office, and the company is traditional, conservative, and offers paid benefits, you might enjoy the perks even though the work is repetitive and routine.

Or you may want to match your skills to a rapidly changing, visionary company hiring you for your imagination and creativity, but offering few benefits. Personality and abilities tests are about making the best-fit match. The tests are matchmakers.

That's why, to prepare for tests, you need to list your values and qualifications, and match them against what the company offers and needs. It's a list of pros and cons that you weigh. The best way to take a corporate test is to turn it into a matchmaking test. It's all because corporations have attitudes. Observe the diagnostic tools in the book *The Character of a Corporation: How Your Company's Culture Can Make or Break Your Business* by Rob Goffee and Lehman B. Fletcher. The character of a corporation is the culture of a corporation, and it sets the bottom line.

There are organizations that emphasize security, routine, and belonging. And then there are their opposites: organizations that emphasize innovation, creativity, and constant change.

According to *The Character of a Corporation*, just as people, companies, and teams come in compulsive and impulsive types. Corporate tests that profile personalities reveal how important it is to match a compulsive routine-seeking job hunter who offers dependability, loyalty, service, and duty with the same type of employer.

What Magazines Does Your Employer Read?

Before you take a corporate test, ask your boss who will be in charge of your career track. What magazines do the company's president and your potential supervisor subscribe to? Change-oriented or traditional publications? Compulsive or impulsive magazines? Does your future employer enjoy science fiction as inspiration? Or does the employer read historical polls and magazines emphasizing successful ventures throughout history?

Find out whether the publications your employer reads are impulsive and futurist or compulsive such as the mainstream, traditional business and historically oriented magazines including *Forbes, Fortune,* and the *Saturday Evening Post.* In addition, almost every industry has its own compulsive and impulsive publications.

Impulsive vs. Compulsive Organizations

The compulsive company emphasizes the security of belonging to a large, solvent firm offering steady work. Routine isn't seen as stressful while climbing the corporate ladder. (Examples include hospitals, government, schools, and the military.)

Equally important for the applicant who is often impulsive is to be matched with an independent, change-oriented, and innovative employer. The impulsive company emphasizes time flexibility and nonlinear fast tracks to the top. Advancement in an impulsive organization is based on ingenuity, inventiveness, and change.

Examples of impulsive organizations include cutting-edge technology and medical research corporations. Compulsive companies include banks, utilities companies, law enforcement, computer security, accounting/auditing firms, electronic systems suppliers, the electronic home response industry, home healthcare software suppliers, government, military service, education, shipping, and the more traditional computer manufacturers such as IBM.

Traditional vs. Change-Oriented Corporations

Is a corporation testing you for compulsive or impulsive work styles? According to *The Character of a Corporation*, compulsive trade publications follow the industrial or technological giants more than the independent company spin-offs.

Impulsive trade journals (historical, poll-taking publications) and similar people-polling periodicals follow the smaller, one-person startup companies, the independents, and new technologies that compete with the giants.

How can you tell whether your organization is impulsive and change-oriented, or compulsive and traditional? Ask yourself the following six questions to gain perspective on whether your own personality matches the values and goals of a traditional or change-oriented company:

1. Does the corporation emphasize utility?

2. Does the company emphasize pitfalls to avoid?

3. Is the company making the equivalent of the safety pin?

4. Does the firm look back in time to tradition in order to move forward new technology?

5. Does the company run a tight ship?

6. Are practical applications emphasized over abstract, theoretical ideas?

If you answered yes to these questions, chances are your organization is compulsive and benchmarking. Your personality profile ends up in commercial databases.

Forward-looking, change-oriented corporations read magazines with content that contains futuristic studies along with material on hidden and niche markets. Content focuses more on insight, vision, and foresight than on hindsight and pitfalls to avoid. These types of corporations rely more on impulse.

Compulsive, traditional organizations focus on fact-checking and historical information that warns of pitfalls to avoid and hindsight based on experience of what worked well in the past and still works. It's as if the bean counters look to people polling and history for facts.

Successful giant industries throughout history are studied—from the Roman Empire's engineering strategies to modern giant industries that are still expanding, and increasing revenue and production.

These are industries people without technical knowledge can understand, industries that produce the necessities of life. Examples include Warren Buffett's investments.

Impulsive corporations, in contrast, include high-technology and genomic corporations on the cutting edge of science and business that people without technical knowledge wouldn't understand so quickly. Microsoft is an example of a forward-looking company.

Imagination-centric and creative imagination-focused companies look forward to new trends for additional signs of rapid change. A new fashion repeated becomes a trend. Impulsive companies may come from business, science, education, technology, art, entertainment, or human resources.

Ask yourself the following six questions to gain perspective on whether your personality matches the values and goals of an imagination-focused company:

1. Does the organization profit by selling imagination?
2. Does it promote both escape and learning as entertainment?
3. Does the organization fulfill consumer needs by offering education as fun?
4. Can the creative employees work flexible hours?
5. Is constant change the company's mission?
6. Are people hired for their intelligence, creativity, and innovation?

If you answered yes to these questions, chances are your organization is impulsive and visionary. Corporate testing is changing the way people learn and play.

Your Boss Wants to Know What Makes You Tick

Corporate testing encourages discussion regarding differences between team members. Personality assessments are catalogued. Your boss wants to know what makes you tick. Will you answer truthfully? Do you know why you chose specific answers?

Take a practice test alone before taking one with your team. What do you want to reveal about yourself to your team, to a company database or scoring center, and to your employer? Can your personality profiling or "good" decision-making assessment scores be used against you even though you're told there are no right or wrong responses (as there are when taking intelligence tests)?

Of course, if your name is on the test and the details remain in your corporation's human resources department's databases, you're identified. If scoring is done by number and not name, there may be a cross-reference index of numbers that match names.

Do you worry about the information being insecure if someone with a laptop takes the information home and the computer is suddenly missing? How do you know whether your personal information will remain confidential or be sold to a marketing or insurance company or the government—except on the word of your employer?

Those are questions that go through the minds of some of those who take corporate tests, but should you care? After all, do you care when a football player scores a 6 or a 50 on a Wonderlic intelligence test? Does it matter whether that is news broadcasted in mainstream media or on the Web? Can you check any given media source for validity or credibility?

What do you think when you read that a test coach hired by an agent trained some of the contenders in a football draft on how to take an intelligence test? Should your test scores and those of celebrities be confidential? Or is it better to know that many football players are very intelligent as well as athletic? It does set a great example for children who enjoy sports such as football and need more motivation to work smarter in school. After all, learning and life are connected.

Testing for Teamwork

Corporate testing emphasizes the think-tank quality of a team. Teams are *partnerships* in brainstorming. Trust, commitment, and simplicity are necessary for teams to move forward with decisions, plans, and actions. Team members don't like complex solutions to problems that teams are asked to solve.

Do corporate tests reveal whether or not team members have the same universal values? Will the tests reveal which team members are benchmarking and which are visionary?

What if the company is a benchmarking or visionary corporation that wants to hire only members who, as the founder is, are either benchmarking or visionary? Will the "differing" team member be singled out as a loose cannon and kept doing busywork, even at the executive level?

Personality assessments can reveal whether team members are making "good" or "bad" decisions. But is there agreement on the team regarding what decisions are right or wrong? Is there a classification system, catalog, or indexed database for good decisions?

The reason for corporate testing in the first place is to have a system that works. Employers need a reliable, time-tested system to turn to when problems need to be solved and results measured.

Bosses make the conceptual leap that because a system is needed for problem-solving in all other aspects of running a business, then corporate tests are the best instruments for team-building. Corporations switch to a corporate test brand that solves specific team-related problems and reveals measurable results.

Team members point out differences rather than similarities. There's no way all members of a team can consistently show only similarities on corporate assessments of personality and decision-making. If corporations are looking for intelligence test scores, they vary from day to day with the same person. Employers have to decide whether to hire those who score high on emotional and social intelligence and those with the highest intelligence test (IQ) scores. Of course, it depends on the nature of the work.

Commitment Through Corporate Testing

What corporate testing is trying to achieve from a team is commitment. The goal of a corporate team is action. Think of the team as the characters in a novel that must move the action forward to a conclusion—a decision and plan. The corporate test is the vehicle that transports the team towards the action.

You can look at the corporate personality test as one solution to the problem of how to organize your plan of action and your decisions. The tests help to organize the entire team's plans based on logically evaluating decisions.

Some individuals will evaluate decisions based on empathy. Others will evaluate decisions based on personal likes or dislikes. And some will evaluate decisions based on a list of pros weighed against cons, only to go with the longer column.

Once every detail falls into its place, plans can move forward to the conclusion. Corporate testing works as a three-act drama: The corporate test is Act I. The individual test results are Act II. And the final act moves decisions into action.

That final act or end result requires commitment from each member on the team. Action is broken down into little baby steps.

Environments of Trust

The role of the test administrator or test-taking coach is to create an environment where trust increases not only between team members, but also between the test coach and the team members. The only way such an environment can grow in a corporation is by detailed interpretation of the test results which are explained further in coursework. Trust also must develop between the test coach and boss or agent who hired the corporate testing coach.

If you're a test coach, you have to battle the books calling some aspects of corporate test taking a cult of personality, the magazine articles pointing out how many different answers people receive when they take certain types of personality tests more than once, and the need for mentorship programs with individualized sessions. You have to persuade the corporation that hired you to let you coach the team.

Corporate testing is not only about trends, it's about learning various emotional intelligence behaviors. Some bosses don't like pop psychology and the spiritual traditions brought into their corporations.

When corporate testing is done to move action forward and develop trust among team members, employers don't always want to hear sermons on transformation or transpersonal psychology. That's too abstract. Facts are wanted. Practical solutions, not abstract theories, are wanted in corporate testing, coaching, and coursework.

The bottom line is if the team members don't trust the corporation and its leaders, how will they learn to trust one another, make commitments, and accept different points of view? Teams have life spans. Teams also outlast the work-life spans of individuals in the groups, and team members are regularly replaced.

Tests for Honestry/Integrity

One type of personality survey is the test for integrity or honesty, usually given to job applicants in service and retail settings, but may be given to any employee where honesty is counted on foremost among workers, managers, and customers.

Employers will hire the person who strongly agrees with total honesty, regardless of the temptations—and strongly disagrees with anything that even hints of dishonest possibilities. To answer questions on a test of honesty/integrity, be sure to strongly agree or strongly disagree. On honesty tests, there are no shades of gray. The act is either honest or dishonest.

When asked whether you'd turn in a fellow employee you caught stealing, the answer managers want to see is yes/strongly agree. There's no such thing as being a 'snitch.' Your total loyalty is to the company at all times, not to friendships formed with co-workers who are dishonest.

Management assumes you'd choose your friends from among the honest workers, not the thieves. Management insists that you believe that most people are honest by nature. Otherwise, there wouldn't be any stores still operating if most people were thieves.

So answer honestly, and keep in mind that your loyalty always would be to the corporation. The applicant hired will be the individual looking for anything suspicious that diminished the company's inventory, sanitation, or income. Watch for trick questions.

Understanding Honesty Tests

Normally, you'd use your discretion to determine and discern shades of gray in answers because you're not a robot or computer. However, the company wants a strongly agree or strongly disagree answer to illustrate your integrity and honesty. In theory, answers depend upon circumstances, but in business, total loyalty to the company is required, which means honesty.

Your answers should always strongly agree or disagree except in any place where human discretion is required to weigh loyalty to the company against loyalty to the co-worker. Human beings normally consider both the circumstances and the evidence before judging whether to obey rules to the letter or break them when safety is in question.

As far as honesty/integrity questions, you're expected to show total loyalty to the organization and not to your co-workers. You'll be hired if an employer can be assured of your commitment, values, and concern at work for the safety and health of the employees. You're hired if you pose the least risk to your employer. Ultimately, you're hired to increase the company's profit and represent the company's image.

Sample Honesty Test

Answer each of the 25 questions by checking one box:

❏ I strongly agree　　❏ I agree　　❏ I disagree　　❏ I strongly disagree

When finished, add up the strongly agree and strongly disagree answers to get your score.

1. If a wallet with identification, credit cards, and $200 in cash is purposely left on the sidewalk by a newspaper reporter to see whether it will be returned as found with the cash and credit cards, most people would be honest enough to immediately return the wallet to its owner.

    ❏ I strongly agree　　❏ I agree　　❏ I disagree　　❏ I strongly disagree

2. Very few people ever have taken anything that didn't belong to them because they understand there are boundaries of ownership that are not to be crossed for any reason.

    ❏ I strongly agree　　❏ I agree　　❏ I disagree　　❏ I strongly disagree

3. You can trust the majority of people.

    ❏ I strongly agree　　❏ I agree　　❏ I disagree　　❏ I strongly disagree

4. Most shoplifters are children.

❏ I strongly agree   ❏ I agree   ❏ I disagree   ❏ I strongly disagree

5. Children who take money or jewelry from a friend's house should be made to apologize, return the item, earn money doing chores or community service, and buy that friend a similar gift.

❏ I strongly agree   ❏ I agree   ❏ I disagree   ❏ I strongly disagree

6. No one I knew as a child or adolescent shoplifted.

❏ I strongly agree   ❏ I agree   ❏ I disagree   ❏ I strongly disagree

7. It's very important that parents and teachers reward children for being honest.

❏ I strongly agree   ❏ I agree   ❏ I disagree   ❏ I strongly disagree

8. Most parents think that it's normal for children to steal small toys that the parents cannot afford.

❏ I strongly agree   ❏ I agree   ❏ I disagree   ❏ I strongly disagree

9. If someone says he or she has never stolen or shoplifted, I naturally believe the person.

❏ I strongly agree   ❏ I agree   ❏ I disagree   ❏ I strongly disagree

10. Shoplifting laws are too lenient.

❏ I strongly agree   ❏ I agree   ❏ I disagree   ❏ I strongly disagree

11. Shoplifters should be punished with long-term jail time.

❏ I strongly agree   ❏ I agree   ❏ I disagree   ❏ I strongly disagree

12. It's okay to buy stolen merchandise if you can get it cheap at a thrift store.

❏ I strongly agree   ❏ I agree   ❏ I disagree   ❏ I strongly disagree

13. Everyone I know is honest.

❏ I strongly agree   ❏ I agree   ❏ I disagree   ❏ I strongly disagree

14. If you're undercharged, it's okay to not bring it to the attention of the management.

❏ I strongly agree   ❏ I agree   ❏ I disagree   ❏ I strongly disagree

15. If you take office supplies home, it's okay because you're probably underpaid.

❏ I strongly agree   ❏ I agree   ❏ I disagree   ❏ I strongly disagree

16. Everybody steals pencils and pens from the boss.

❏ I strongly agree   ❏ I agree   ❏ I disagree   ❏ I strongly disagree

17. It's acceptable to steal time by leaving the office early when there's no work to do.

❏ I strongly agree   ❏ I agree   ❏ I disagree   ❏ I strongly disagree

18. It's proper to call in sick when you're healthy and just want to go to a movie or the beach.

    ❐ I strongly agree   ❐ I agree   ❐ I disagree   ❐ I strongly disagree

19. Everybody steals something at work—time, days off, or office supplies.

    ❐ I strongly agree   ❐ I agree   ❐ I disagree   ❐ I strongly disagree

20. I strongly agree that finders are keepers of anything found in public places.

    ❐ I strongly agree   ❐ I agree   ❐ I disagree   ❐ I strongly disagree

21. If my boss sends me a paycheck with more money than I earned, I'll keep it without bringing the error to my boss's attention.

    ❐ I strongly agree   ❐ I agree   ❐ I disagree   ❐ I strongly disagree

22. It's okay to take a week off from work for my honeymoon by calling in sick.

    ❐ I strongly agree   ❐ I agree   ❐ I disagree   ❐ I strongly disagree

23. If I see my supervisor stealing, I'll tell my co-workers, but not inform the company headquarters in another city.

    ❐ I strongly agree   ❐ I agree   ❐ I disagree   ❐ I strongly disagree

24. If a co-worker uses illegal drugs on the job, it's right to report it to the boss, even though I'll probably be sabotaged by my co-workers for snitching.

    ❐ I strongly agree   ❐ I agree   ❐ I disagree   ❐ I strongly disagree

25. Employees who take home dog food without permission from discount stores are not really stealing if they donate the pet food to feed dogs owned by elderly shut-ins who are delivered hot meals.

    ❐ I strongly agree   ❐ I agree   ❐ I disagree   ❐ I strongly disagree

Scoring

With an honesty test, the scoring is simple: A 100 percent score indicates the test-taker's total honesty. Lesser scores question the honesty factor.

Corporate Tests of Values

Corporations want to measure your ability to follow rules and directions. Values, intelligence, job skills, and health are measurable by corporations to get or keep a job. Whatever job you take, your work is about problem-solving. Either you help people solve their problems, or you solve problems with data or machines. For example, there's a proposition on the Wal-Mart survey that "rules have to be followed to the letter at all times." You're measured on whether you answer that you agree "strongly," "very strongly," or "totally." Rules are interpreted with "discretion," according to author Barbara Ehrenreich in her 2001 book, *Nickel and Dimed*. Ehrenreich went through personality survey testing at Wal-Mart, as she reports in her book about what it's like working at entry-level jobs that pay at or close to the minimum wage.

With pre-employment personality tests or surveys such as the Wal-Mart survey given when you apply for entry-level jobs, corporations may have personnel assistants, clerks, or retail supervisors administer tests that are scored by computers. Although there are no right or wrong answers, what the tests measure your ability to follow test proposition rules.

Some tests measure honesty. Corporations want to know if you can follow directions. If you deviate from company rules, policies, or procedures, you could be considered a loose cannon. At the executive level, there are tests measuring creativity and innovation.

For many workers, not only corporate tests have to be taken, but physical exams must be passed, including blood and urine tests for drug use. Many companies require medical exams in order to get health insurance coverage. For some jobs, a physical exam is required before being employed such as a TB patch test for teachers, nurses, educational aides, gerontology workers, and others working closely with people. Corporations may measure your emotional investments.

Understanding Values Tests

To take a "values" assessment, you begin by making a list of the concepts that have measurable worth to you. These are concepts that you choose when dealing with details of the day. Your value choices determine how you live your life.

There's a test for almost anything that can be measured. Values can be measured as principles or beliefs in which you have an emotional investment. Employers use values assessments as indicators of future job performance.

Some values tests simply ask you to rank your values. Other tests define "life priority" values. The premise is that values, unconsciously or not, still govern actions and determine life goals.

Indicators of future job performance designed for managers and sales personnel also are given to all levels of workers. Some questions asked on values assessments measure whether you are self assured, responsible, emotional stable, cautious, and original in your thinking.

The assessments question you on how you might handle personal relations. Values tests look at how high your self-esteem scores. How do you feel about your boss measuring your office or factory vigor, enthusiasm, or charisma?

Some values assessments ask you to arrange relationship problems in a prioritized, step-by-step list or map. For questions about honesty, multiple-choice answers require you to make a choice. You'll create a plan that you and team members can follow to get a handle on people problems. Basically, on a values assessment, you'll be using your values at work to make choices.

The values measured by these types of assessments include choices that reveal your values concerning honesty, self-control, and equality. Values assessments also measure self-respect, goal orientation, independence, altruism, and social support systems.

If you're a manager, chances are your boss will give you a values assessment to see how well you solve, prioritize, or handle problems that come up daily in your relationships with co-workers. If you're an entry-level job applicant, a values assessment emphasizes choices you make about honesty, work relationships, and company procedures.

The values assessment you take usually comes with a personality questionnaire, indicator, or classifier. One example of a values test published by a British company, is a short indicator of future performance called Global Gordon's Personal Profile Inventory (Global GPP-I) distributed by ASE Psychometric Tests in London (*www.ase-solutions.co.uk/product.asp?id=34*). The indicator assesses nine major areas of personality dimensions that have been identified as important indicators of future job performance. These areas are ascendancy, (or self assuredness), responsibility, emotional stability, cautiousness, original thinking, personal relations, vigor, and self-esteem.

The Global GPP-I scores quickly. According the ASE Website, the assessment is "particularly suitable for the recruitment of sales personnel and sales and general managers." The assessment is not timed and takes about 20 minutes to complete.

The United States has a wide variety of similar tests, and some large corporations have their own values assessments. In San Antonio, Texas, Harcourt Assessment Incorporated's Values Arrangement List (VAL) is an online survey to accurately measure personal values. VAL overcomes this limitation by using advanced statistical methods and test design to generate an in-depth, easy-to-understand Individual Feedback Report.

According to the Harcourt Assessment, Inc. Website (*harcourtassessment.com*), VAL is used to "Assist individuals in understanding their value system for the purpose of ensuring their fit within a job or organization, help guide individuals toward better self-understanding, control, and responsibility based upon their value system, and begin the process of defining and refining individuals' career and life plans based on their value system."

So, we come across the word *system* again. In the corporate world, everything needs a system to function. And all systems need plans. Executives like systems to control, organize, and categorize people, products, and services. If values guide your behavior, then there is a system for assessing values.

Values Guide Your Behavior

What do you value? Values are principles you use to guide your behavior. What is a particular value worth to you? Your values also determine how you treat people who have no power to promote, represent, or connect you, such as janitorial or food service personnel and strangers you meet on the road.

Your values also reveal your behavior towards others when no one else is looking. How do your values compare to your personal likes and dislikes? How do you measure worth? How do you prioritize and compare your values? Do you share those values with your social group? Or are your values individual?

Values are divided into the tangible (physical) and intangible (emotional). You have an emotional investment in your values. Some people also have an emotional investment in those values of their social group, such as defending their social group's honor. Is a value an act, an emotion, or a behavior?

It's a belief in which you have an emotional investment. A tangible value is measured by how much that value is worth to you. Intangible values also have measurable worth to the individual. Your belief, idea, or choice can be for or against someone else's belief, idea, or choice. Examples of values include commitment to family, faith, profession, and simplicity. Simplicity means that what you value gives you all the answers you were looking for in your life in the immediate world around you.

Your values determine your behavior. For example, what you believe to be honesty is how you will be behave when faced with a situation where you could choose two courses of action. If you have the opportunity to pocket an overpayment, would you, or would you takes the steps to refund the overpayment to a customer? These tests attempt to determine what your likely behavior would be based on your values.

? ? ? ? ? ? ? ?

Chapter 5

Test Scoring: What They Mean, and How They Influence Hiring

Interestingly, your values may be influenced by physical and environmental circadian rhythms. A circadian rhythm is a roughly-24-hour cycle in the physiological processes of living beings. Commonly referred to as a biological clock, it also refers to the light needed, as well as sleep required, to reset the internal clock. If you hire a test-taking coach for improving performance on intelligence tests and tests of job-related skills, you might consider hiring a biorhythms coach to find out which are your best days physiologically for taking any type of assessments. You might wish to time the Monday slumps and the Wednesday jumps of your inner clocks.

Understanding Biorhythms

If you are going to take any type of corporate test, you might want to take into consideration your biorhythms and perhaps hire a biorhythms coach to help you find out when your body is best prepared for any lengthy corporate testing.

Chronobiology is the medical term for biorhythm/internal clock theory. (Biorhythms measure the physical, emotional and intellectual cycles, whereas internal clocks measure mood, memory, and body temperature over a 24-hour cycle.) Every person has a built-in biological clock regulating the levels of various hormones and the rates or chemical processes in response to internal and environmental cues. Individuals respond to this regulation by periodic changes in their growth and behavior patterns. (Jet lag is an example of what happens when an internal clock is out of whack.)

There is no aspect of human biology that is not influenced by your daily internal clock rhythms. This, in turn, influences the way in which you conduct our daily business.

Your blood pressure rises between 8:00 a.m. and 12 noon, and then starts dropping until its midnight low. There's an internal clock governing our hormone levels and our heartbeat, all following different clocks that may bear only a slight relation to our daily cycle.

The best predictor of job performance is body temperature. As it falls from a 10 p.m. zenith of 99 degrees to a pre-dawn nadir of 97 degrees, your mental functions drop. You perform best when all your body's clocks are in sync. When your mechanisms fall out of step, you make errors or have accidents. So-called "morning people" have a higher body temperature than an afternoon or evening person, which gives them an early-morning energy burst.

For many people, memory peaks at 11 a.m., but math skills drop off at noon. Business performance levels fall just after lunch. By late afternoon, stress can be handled more effectively.

The internal clock is as individual as a fingerprint. What is certain is that the person you are in the morning is different from the one you are at night. Once you have determined what your high and low energy levels are, you will be better able to adjust your prospecting and selling activities to more efficient and profitable time slots.

Administering Corporate Testing

Organizational psychologists may give and/or score corporate assessments. So do career counselors, consultants, coaches, therapists, clergy, job developers, and some trained and authorized human resource managers. Organizational psychologists use their psychology training to train, manage, and develop human resources, also known as personnel management.

According to Money.com's definition of duties of organizational psychologists (*money.cnn.com/magazines/moneymag/bestjobs/snapshots/78.html*), organizational psychologists "apply principles of psychology to personnel, administration, management, sales, and marketing problems. Activities may include policy planning, employee screening, training and development, and organizational development and analysis." The site also reports that organizational psychologists "may work with management to reorganize the work setting to improve worker productivity."

When an organizational psychologist and team give corporate assessments, its aim is to improve worker productivity. In 2006, psychologists' annual pay averaged only $77,734—compared to the annual pay of industrial-organizational psychologists, whose average is reported at $85,109, according to *Money Magazine's* annual "Best Jobs in America" issue (2006), and *Salary.com* (a Website that rates careers on salary and job prospects) by Tara Kalwarski, Daphne Mosher, Janet Paskin and Donna Rosato. The reports of jobs and salaries can be found online at *money.cnn.com/magazines/moneymag/bestjobs/*. Also see the Best Jobs in America

Website (*money.cnn.com/magazines/moneymag/bestjobs/snapshots/78.html*). *Money.com* also reports that 25 percent of organizational psychologists make more than $98,567, with total annual compensation (including bonus) listed as $103,276.

Baby Boomers are starting businesses in record numbers, according to *CNNMoney.com*. Any time a large demographic, such as new retirees, open businesses, a door opens to potential corporate testing administrators to find new clients seeking team-building or leadership training. And along with training often comes corporate assessments used by executives to improve worker productivity. In turn, a door opens for tutors and coaches to help clients prepare for these corporate tests.

Why Corporations Give Abstract Reasoning Tests

Abstract reasoning is another phrase used in the corporate world for critical thinking skills. Executives who work by a system choose abstract reasoning tests because a single assessment can measure *general* ability for most jobs requiring general knowledge and generalist skills.

An abstract reasoning test can be given to almost anyone applying for any type of job that requires broad and shallow skills. Generalist skills can be transferred easily from one type of industry to another.

Generalist skills don't become obsolete quickly. They include making people feel comfortable in a corporate setting and presenting a favorable image of a particular corporation and its products to customers. Some services are specialist—such as a computer repair technician. Other services are generalist, such as a customer service representative.

Generalist skills are about explaining—making complex material easy to understand by users of a product. Three examples of different generalist skills are trade-show event planner, administrative assistant, and general sales manager.

In contrast, if your job requires vertical in-depth "specialist" skills, you'll probably receive a separate skills test to see whether your specialist skills meet the company's requirements to perform the particular job. Three examples of different specialist skills are accident reconstruction photographer, patterns recognition computer scientist, and forensic geneticist. In the publishing world, editors and proofreaders usually are given separate editing, grammar, and spelling tests along with a proofreading proficiency test.

An editor might also have to take a Miller Analogy Test. If your corporation requires you to take the Miller Analogy Test for any reason, see the "How to Ace the Miller Analogy Test" Website (*www.milleranalogytest.com/*). This abilities test usually is given to graduate-school applicants, but also may be given by corporations in communications industries and by non-profits.

According to the Miller Analogy Test Website, a problem most test-takers face is the lack of a "critical word strength" when doing math problems. Another big problem with some tests is the time management mental obstacles that a test throws at you. Corporate tests require you to *analyze*. What's your logical system? How does your system compare to the test's system? If your boss gives you an abstract reasoning test, it is to measure your general ability. Chances are your job requires critical thinking skills, and there are lots of college courses in critical thinking.

You'll take a test of abstract reasoning if the job you're hired to do and the people you will manage require dealing with abstract concepts. One example is when you apply for a job in technology, such as a phone company switching technician. The job may not deal with abstract ideas, but the intelligence (process) needed to handle the practical details is measured by an abstract reasoning test.

How to Practice for an Abstract Reasoning Test

Here's how to break down any abstract thinking test to its bare bones parts.

1. List the rules.

2. Identify the symbols.

3. Identify any parts.

4. Reduce these parts.

5. List what the parts represent.

6. Look for repeating patterns or sequences.

If you get stuck, go back to listing the rules. Identify the symbols. Then look for a repeating sequence.

Keep repeating these steps as if they were a loop that returns to the first step. All the information and rules usually are given in the *first* step. The technique is to pare everything in the test question to its bare bones. The goal is to recognize patterns.

Design Your Own Test Questions

In a corporate setting, practicing abstract reasoning means designing your own questions. The critical thinking process forces you to keep going back to the first rules—the first information given. Practice taking abstract thinking tests that you find in magazines, books, and newspapers. A symbol can stand for a mock-language word or a rule. The symbols can be anything from words and numbers to geometric forms.

Taking the Aptitude Test

Out of the 4,000–5,000 corporate tests given to measure emotional intelligence, advanced knowledge of a subject, job skills, personality, control, caution, and even potential for domestic violence, only about 50 human capacities and aptitudes tests measure cognitive abilities (intelligence), according to business psychologist Dr. Mark Parkinson, in his book, *How to Master Psychometric Tests*. Abilities tests measure thinking. And thinking, according to Parkinson, is divided into abstract, verbal, numerical, perceptual, spatial, or mechanical.

Let's add one more type of thinking: clerical, because clerical performance assessments are given on so many entry-level tests for administrative assistant and records clerk job applicants. High schools used to give courses in "clerical practice" and "record-keeping" to business students who didn't take algebra and college-preparatory courses. Clerical skills assessments fall under aptitude testing. These tests usually consist of filing, spelling, and arithmetic assessments.

If you're applying for a job as a file clerk, you'll most likely receive two tests: one for clerical skills on how to check information for accuracy, and another for reading and math skills, such as an intelligence test (usually the Wonderlic test).

You probably will take a keyboarding speed test to see how fast you type accurately. (The typing speed test comes from the days before computers when clerical workers took tests on typewriters.) Today, it's called keyboarding speed.

Your keystrokes are measured and scored for accuracy and speed. If you're an executive, professional, or manager, instead of a data entry speed and accuracy test on a computer keyboard, you'll probably take abilities or abstract reasoning tests and personality assessments.

Preparing for the Popular Tests

What do you look for when preparing to take some of the most popular tests? Corporations with traditional, conservative characters may choose abilities tests. Corporations with forward-looking visionary goals focused on change and imagination might learn more to personality profiles and decision-making training of teams focused on developing leadership skills in managers.

Before you take corporate tests, ask the particular company which tests are being given. With research you can learn the difference between questionnaires, tests, inventories, assessments, indicators, and classifiers. Who scores the tests? Are they administered by human resource managers, career counselors, organizational psychologists, or others?

By phoning the human resources department you can get a handle on and explore the attitudes and comments about test-taking preparation. All you have to do is get a practice copy of the test or find one online. If the corporation won't let you see the test, ask the name of the test and contact the test publishers for a sample. Also, there are popular corporate sample tests in the back of this book.

Validating the Testing

Most of these tests are scored by previously published material that gives "individually analyzed" insight into how people see themselves. Tests generally are validated by reviewers, and the reviews are published in library journals. You can also read the reviews online. Organizational psychologists who design these instruments often are the reviewers.

Some tests are self-administered. Ask your corporation which behavioral instruments are reliable and used most frequently. Tests also measure how people perceive other people. Many of the popular tests measure emotional maturity—how one behaves under stress in a corporation or under unpredictable conditions.

Skill tests given to firefighters and police offers measure psychological issues concerning how you behave in crises or under stress. Similar stress tests may be given to people who give information to the public and have a high interaction with people of all walks of life on the job. Examples would be bus drivers, customer relations assistants, aircraft controllers, and telephone technical support (people who take calls all day for help on configuring software or setting up appliances).

Besides abilities tests, your company might give you specific job-skill tests, achievement tests, competitive tests, honesty tests, decision-making tests, emotional quotient tests, career area choice tests, personality questionnaires, and aptitude profiling tests for jobs requiring certain attitudes.

Physical tests for extroversion/introversion may include a "self-insight" questionnaire and/or a saliva test which measures increased saliva secretion (introversion) versus dry mouth (extroversion) based on doing rapid hand movement tasks in a group for several minutes. That's why it's important to find out from the HR or educational technology department which batch of tests you'll take.

Each test measures a different trait. Testing could be of emotional maturity. Or anger management and patience. Or abilities tests of math, reading, and spelling. Or job skills if those duties are what your job requires. When you find out what the tests measure and which tests are going to be given to you, use available online practice in taking tests of critical thinking.

Fitting in With the Group vs. Competency

You're hired for two reasons:

1. You pose the least risk to the employer.

2. You fit in with the group.

More people are terminated for personality differences leading to conflicts than for incompetence or tardiness. Corporate testing positions you. What's your number in the queue?

Every advertising agency on Madison Avenue knows that "you don't get a second chance to make a first impression," as stated in the marketing classic, *Positioning: The Battle For Your Mind.* Positioning works the same way for corporate test-takers. On a personality profile, intelligence test, or decision-making assessment, you only get one chance to position your first impression. When your employer sees your corporate test score or position, the first impression is a mirror held up to the company's image.

When an employer looks at your assessment interpretation or results, your boss wants to see similarities of skills, talents, and goals. You either fit into the group or you're an outsider. A corporate test is propaganda. It's a buzz piece of publicity for the company. It's a newswire.

Corporate assessments are designed to manipulate with visual images or words even though no image is on the paper. Using only words, you have to create a visual image before you can make a decision on a personality preference or a timed decision.

Did you forget vital information in the short time allowed to make a good decision? How does the assessment define a "good" decision if there is no right or wrong answer on personality profiling assessments or decision-making timed questionnaires and classifiers? Your personality may be regulated by your genes. But your values are influenced by your culture and early family life.

? ? ? ? ? ? ? ?

Chapter 6

Why Tests Are Used

Employers count on corporate assessments to reduce risk, wasted time, and fiscal insecurities related to human resources. Abilities tests, often given along with personality profiles, measure abstract reasoning measures and cognitive intelligence. Abilities tests measure job skills and/or intellectual reasoning abilities or "critical thinking."

You can practice taking free IQ tests online that give you a lot of exercise in discerning shapes, sizes, colors, and numbers of features on an object. (You can quickly find tests by using any search engine and entering "free IQ tests.") There also are emotional quotient (EQ) intelligence tests online.

Employers may think corporate testing results are absolute truth, but the history of test design shows errors and inconsistencies. Tests are thought to give employers the promise and prospect of employees with the potential to perform at or even beyond human limits. The problem is that tests are designed by humans and may, or may not, be rife with human error. There are, however, popular corporate tests highly recommended that have stood up to the test of time.

These assessments are reviewed often for consistency. Only by reading the test reviews can you begin to see what professional test designers are looking for in a corporate assessment. Check out some at the Tickle Test Website (*web.tickle.com/*). Some online tests are for entertainment purposes. What do professionals think of a particular test? Are the scores accurate? A score also may depend upon how you feel when you take the test.

The thinking practice comes in handy when you take a variety of the free IQ and EQ tests online and give your mind a workout looking for patterns. Abilities tests are mostly about seeing what symbols, words, or numbers have in common. Once you've observed the pattern, the next step is to draw a circle or make a mental note of how the objects, numbers, or words are grouped together. You organize like objects with like objects in your mind.

Look for patterns that keep repeating. Think of an abilities test as a song that repeats the chorus in your head with similar patterns, words, numbers, or objects. Some of those objects will repeat in patterns or groups that you can organize into pairs or threes or fours. Some objects are organized on the diagonal. Others you imagine you're looking down from above at a telephone pole in the ground and picture what you see from the top as a bird's eye view. It looks to be a circle from above.

There's a lot of shifting shapes or rotating them, but you won't have to flip over objects on most tests. Look for squares that progress from left to right or right to left. With words, substitute made-up words for real language. Do objects, numbers, or words move from bottom to top in a repeating pattern? To score a correct answer, you have to predict what's missing from a sequence. There is logic in the patterns of an abilities test.

You'll usually be asked to find the next one, two, or three words, numbers, or symbols in a sequence—or find the missing symbol, word, or number in a sequence or pattern. That's why all these free online IQ tests are good to take for practice. Even if you think the score is for entertainment purposes only, you get the chance to repeat and practice thinking in the logic of abstract patterns.

$$?$$

2 Examples of Abstract Reasoning

Question #1: What are the next two symbols in the sequence?
   $\in \Omega \prod \in \partial \prod \in \Omega \prod \in$? ?

   a. $\in$
   b. Ω
   c. ∂
   d. $\prod$

Answering Question #1
   The answer that would fill in the two question marks of Question #1 is (c.) ∂ and (d.) $\prod$. Why? Look question #1. Are the symbols are of equal size? No. "D" is larger than "c" and "b." You need to rule out first that what the test wants you to look for is not the smallest object or symbol. Once size is ruled out, next look for patterns of repetition.

   Your search for a pattern, sequence, or group will tell you that the $\in$ (a) keeps going right after $\prod$ (d) so that the other two symbols, Ω and ∂, both alternate their patterns or sequences. Remember that in a corporate test of abstract thinking, instead of symbols or geometric forms, anything else may be used, such as pictures, words, colors, sounds, fabrics, photos, sculptures, vials of liquid, scents, or textures.

Tests of reasoning are either asking you to find the smallest or largest symbol or to find out what the pattern of repetition or sequence is. The answer is what makes the most important difference in the pattern. The repetition sequence is more important than the size of the objects in this case. You're not asked to do any counting or math. You are asked to find a pattern related to sequence of repetition. Even this test represents a system.

The abstract thinking test may relate to products that your corporation produces. Usually, a standardized test published by a testing company is used. There may be one test for entry-level job applicants and another for executives. What they have in common is that they follow a specific system of testing.

Analyzing Question #1

Look at the Ω (b). There are two of the same symbol Ω. One Ω falls in second place. The other Ω falls in eighth place. There is only one ∂ (c). This (c) symbol ∂ is placed at position number five in the first row of example one. Look at it, and observe that's it's the *only symbol of its kind.* There's no other ∂ symbol.

Keep observing the details. You'll soon see that there are two (b)s ΩΩ and one (c) ∂. So the next symbols in the logical pattern or sequence have to be ∂ (c) followed by ∏ (d).

Question #2: What's the missing symbol?

∈ Ω ∏
Ω ∏ ∈
∏ ∈ ?

    a. ∈
    b. Ω
    c. ∏
    d. ∂

Answering Question #2

The answer is (b). Look for a repeating pattern or sequence. The example uses the sequence or pattern of numbers 2, 1, and 3—that is, you have the 2, 1, 3 sequence in the answer.

The answer is the missing sequence, which is simply number 3—Ω—in the 2, 1, 3 sequence. In this abstract reasoning test, an object or symbol is substituted for the missing object you must insert to complete the pattern. Picture a weave pattern. What's missing is that Ω needs to be inserted in third place (where the question mark is). It is inserted in the third row in the third place. That's the sequence: 2, 1, 3.

If you pictured Ω as the color blue, and the other symbols as the colors green (Π) and white ($\in$), then the answer would be a striped woven cloth. The pattern would look this way: Π green, $\in$ white, and Ω blue. Whether the abstract reasoning abilities test pattern is represented as symbols, colors, numbers, words, or any other object, you're looking for repeating patterns or sequences much the same as you'd look for the pattern in a woven fabric, such as a sweater or carpet.

Analyzing Question #2

Observe what's going on in the horizontal rows. You only have three symbols to work with in the first two columns. Logically, the three symbols follow in order as a 2, 1, 3 sequences. There's no chaos here, nothing out of place. But there's no chronological order. Instead you have a pattern or sequence like a repeating weave of fabric in the horizontal rows. It's not a linear count in place, as in 1, 2, 3. Instead, the sequence or pattern is 2, 1, 3.

Note that the symbols appear once in each row except for the Ω symbol, which appears twice followed by the third row, where Ω is missing from third place, where it logically is supposed to be. Instead there's a question mark in that place. There is a numerical pattern or sequence. In this example, it is not the simple 1, 2, 3 sequence that is played out. Instead it's the 2, 1, 3 pattern that is not linear.

Note that Ω (b) follows $\in$ (a), and Π (c) follows (b). So patterns do not have to be linear in order to repeat a sequence. Music is one example where sequences repeat but are not chronological. One doesn't have to be followed by two. Two can be followed by one, or any other number sequence.

In the abstract thinking required on this test, you make the conceptual leap of logic that the missing symbol is (b) Ω. Why is the missing symbol (b) Ω? Let's slow it down and take it one step at a time to see the pattern.

First, look at the observable sequence. The observable sequence is (b) followed by (a) followed by (c)—or 2, followed by 1, followed by 3. Practice the various ways your mind reaches the same answer. Fiddle logically and creatively with the ways that come to mind just to practice observing patterns and sequences while looking at symbols.

In the practice session, detailing and observing the logic, pattern, and chronological or repetitive sequences are ways to arrive at the answer. The other way to study pattern recognition is through creative imagination—going on a tangent. Some universities offer Ph.D.'s in pattern recognition, usually through their computer science, physics, math, or life sciences departments. Humans always have been better than computers in recognizing certain patterns, so far, especially patterns in human faces, body language, and gestures.

On a corporate abilities test, you are timed, and need simple, quick answers. Here's how you use the fast-track logic. Note that this symbol, Ω appears in the first row. That symbol also is placed second in the second row. You're looking at the rows horizontally. Each row consists of three symbols, except for the final row. The last row contains only two symbols and a question mark.

Your goal—the answer—is to find out which symbol the question mark represents. You know that the final row has a missing symbol that is replaced by a question mark. You check again that each row above the last row has only three symbols.

In the first row, the symbol Ω is placed second in a sequence/pattern. In the second row, the symbol Ω is placed first in the sequence. And in the third row the symbol Ω doesn't appear at all. It's missing from the third row. It's replaced by the question mark. You fill in the answer where the question mark is by choosing the correct letter.

Therefore, Ω (b) is the missing symbol that now appears as number three in place in the third position in sequence in the last row. Thus, you see the pattern sequence is 2, 1, and 3. In row one, Ω is second.

In row two, Ω is first in the sequence. And in the last row, Ω has to be in third place. You see how the pattern 2, 1, 3 falls into logical place? The question mark at the end of horizontal row three is in the third place, where the Ω symbol logically must fall. Thus, Ω (b) is the correct answer.

The pattern or sequence for the three rows is 2, 1, 3. In different questions, this pattern could repeat as 2, 1, 3 or change on another question to the chronological, linear 1, 2, 3, or to any other sequence of numbers, words, or symbols.

Picture yourself with knitting needles. We'll use the names of knitting stitches as an example. If 2 is perl, 1 is knit, and 3 is crochet, then that pattern as a specific, repeated sequence would play out in three dimensions. The result could be music, a weaving pattern of a carpet, or a sweater. You'd see a pattern. It's all about pattern recognition skills.

$$?$$

Preparing for Verbal Assessments

Verbal tests are given in corporate settings in order to see how well you follow instructions or directions. To prepare for any type of verbal assessment, play Scrabble. Word games stimulate your verbal reasoning abilities by giving you practice in recognizing, using, and understanding words. Timed, verbal assessments test reading comprehension and your knowledge of spelling, grammar, and word analogies.

Tests may ask you to complete sentences, find a misspelled word, or fix incorrect grammar, such as discerning complete sentences from incomplete and dangling clauses. With reading comprehension assessments, you're examined on how well and how fast you understand passages. Questions relate to the meaning of what happens or what the character does in a stories, business articles, or technical passages. Prepare for these tests by looking up the meaning of words.

Review grammar. Verbal tests measure how well you can manipulate the structure of your language. Grammar is verbal logic.

The best way to prepare for verbal tests is to read a book of practice exercises on grammar, practice playing Scrabble, and read short passages for comprehension from any publication. Then make up five questions that require you to understand the details and the big picture of what you have read. The questions should be based on your reading of the passage.

Time yourself about five to 10 minutes to answer the questions. The Web has several grammar and spelling tutorial sites. Check out the Nonstop English site (*www.nonstopenglish.com/*). Reading comprehension tests score you on the understanding of what you just read. The goal is to measure how well you can follow instructions or directions. Verbal reasoning assessments measure your ability to choose particular words by following directions.

?

Verbal Assessment Example

Which three words in each question do not belong with the other words?

1. a. compunction	2. a. pleat	3. a. hand truck
b. comity	b. pledge	b. dolly
c. cloche	c. tweed	c. wagon
d. beret	d. diptych	d. cart
e. fedora	e. image	e. meter
f. bonnet	f. plush	f. marina
g. dither	g. plait	g. bill
h. snood	h. twist	h. chariot

Answers

Question #1

The three words that do not belong are *compunction, comity,* and *dither*.

If you recognize the patterns and meanings in the words, you'll see that *cloche, beret, bonnet, snood,* and *fedora* are all types of hats or head coverings. *Compunction* and *comity* are nouns unrelated in meaning, although they share a common beginning alphabet letter.

Question #2

The three words that do not belong are *pledge, diptych,* and *image*. The rest of the words refer to types of fabric weaves. *Pleat, tweed, plush, twist,* and *plait* refer to carpet or cloth weaving styles or textures, such as braids, twist, plush, or folds. *Plush* refers to the nap of cloth or carpet.

Question #3

The three words that do not belong are *meter, marina*, and *bill*. The rest of the words refer to similar hand trucks, types of wagons, or carts. A *dolly* is a hand truck, and shopping wagons, chariots, or carts are or were used to transport small, heavy objects by hand. Note all the words are nouns.

?

How to Answer Verbal Reasoning Tests

Answering verbal reasoning tests depends upon your prior dictionary use. Here's where playing Scrabble with a well-used dictionary nearby increases your word recognition pattern reaction time. Practice recognizing similar words, word relationships, and definitions. Most timed verbal reasoning tests are about recognizing patterns, grammar, spelling, and definitions, or measuring reading comprehension skills. Some verbal tests are sentence-completion exercises. Others ask for analogies.

A test of analogies—verbal, numerical, or spatial—measures your ability to compare two different items in order to emphasize a form of similarity. The Miller Analogies Test specifically tests you on comparing different words or items looking for similarity. Nearly all tests measure and score your pattern-recognition skills.

A month before you take a verbal reasoning test, work on daily dictionary readings to enlarge your vocabulary. Learn to recognize similar words, especially nouns. *The Quintessential Dictionary*, by I. Moyer Hunsberger, is very helpful for learning new words used in the business world among executives. The words have appeared in reviews of books, magazines, newspapers, and in other mainstream media sources. The dictionary contains more than 3,000 words you should know to make your writing and speaking elegant, precise, and confident.

Spend 15 minutes daily learning alternative meanings and definitions for words from dictionary and thesaurus readings to enlarge your vocabulary. Play Scrabble to help you make rapid word associations and improve spelling. Learn at least 10 new words per day. Take up origami to exercise your right-brain hemisphere in recognizing and rotating non-verbal shapes.

?

Reading-Comprehension Test Example

Corporate reading-comprehension assessments may ask you questions to test whether you understood the passage you have read. Comprehension questions may require a one-sentence answer, or answers where you check a box labeled "true" or "false." Reading comprehension questions may also be multiple-choice. Some tests have blank spaces or lines where you fill in the answers. Corporate reading-comprehension tests often are online as part of abilities testing.

Reading-comprehension assessments test you on whether you understood what you read. You answer briefly in a sentence or sometimes, with a word or two. Most reading-comprehension assessments are timed. Answer the six reading comprehension questions that follow this sample passage with one complete sentence.

Despite the reality of growing cultural diversity, employers still look for work patterns and values familiar to US corporations. Employers want information they can understand quickly when reading your résumé. The most important heading you can emphasize in a résumé or cover letter is to state your gender in the "Job Overview" section on your résumé. Your interviewer may not know your gender by the spelling or sound of your name. Consider putting Ms. or Mr. with your name on your cover letter.

Picking from among your many abilities is difficult. So list only those skills that are highly valued by the company. Research the company's needs. Look at job descriptions, and briefly explain how your skills apply.

Identify and highlight what you do best in terms of what the employer values most. Focus on an employer's greatest company need. Explain specifically, using details of your skills, how an employer will save time and money by hiring you. Include details regarding how you can solve a specific problem and get results.

Reading-Comprehension Questions
1. How will an employer save time and money by hiring you?

2. How do you use a job description to show that your skills can apply to an employer's needs?

3. What do you focus on to identify an employer's greatest need?

4. What's the most important heading you can emphasize in a resume?

5. What should you identify and highlight on a résumé?

6. What do U.S. employers look for regarding growing cultural diversity in corporations?

Answers
1. By detailing how you can solve a specific problem and get results, you can save an employer time and money.

2. You briefly explain specifically how each of your work skills applies to the employer's job description.

3. Focus on only the skills you have that are highly valued by the company.

4. Putting your gender on your resume by listing Ms. or Mr. before your name is the most important heading you can emphasize on a resume.

5. Identify and highlight what you do best in terms of what the employer values most.

6. Employers look for work patterns and values familiar to U.S. corporations.

?

Predictive Validity of Corporate Tests

What worries people most about taking corporate tests is the predictive validity of the test. Learn as much as you can about the validity of the test before you take it. All the information you need can be obtained from the test publisher, from *Mental Measurements Yearbooks* at the library, from online reviews, and from your human resources department.

Personality is individual. Your character traits are not so generalized that one test fits all known personality profiles. Test designers search for objectivity. Yet personality tests are subjective. Most people don't think much about understanding themselves until they have to take a personality profile.

Test designers usually recommend that you don't exaggerate your personality characteristics, values, or abilities. Questionnaires are supposed to give a fair and balanced assessment of how you match a variety of jobs. Personality assessments given at work are supposed to reveal *typical* corporate-related attitudes and values. The purpose of a corporate test is to see how well you are suited to the tasks and duties of a particular job.

You're supposed to see yourself taking a corporate test to identify further training and job development requirements needed. You're taking tests to understand what resources you use for motivation. Personality tests usually are given along with abilities tests and decision-making assessments. The focus is on leadership training. Skill testing also screens out job applicants.

Test publishers tell you that the purpose of testing at all levels of employment is to identify satisfying work for which you are well-suited.

Today, few strangers have time for informational interviews. So you have to practice by constructing your own tests. You'd need a large sample of people in the specific job you want—say the job of registered representative or stockbroker.

You'd ask your large sample what their attitudes, interests, and values are and what motivates them. You'd list their answers. Then compose questions that fit the replies and could be answered in a 20-minute test.

Understanding Personality Assessments

The following is Anne's August 2006 e-mail interview with Katherine Parramore, Director, Educational Marketing & Strategic Alliances, Alutiiq, LLC, Homeland Security Division, in Vienna, Virginia.

Q: Is there one assessment that fits all? Or do managers get separate tests from administrative assistants?

A: I would be surprised if in the world of "personality" tests people were giving differing assessments to different groups. That invites a "disparate treatment" lawsuit. Aptitude or skills tests (manual dexterity, use of types of computer software programs) are job skills related and therefore permissible.

Q: What do most corporate personality assessments measure?

A: There used to be in an instrument called 'Profiles' that I used back in the 1990s to measure likelihood of success in *functional* areas/skills, based on a database of the skills people had possessed that were previously successful in the same role. But you can have all the appropriate skills and not be motivated to use them or have a work environment that doesn't provide the resources for functionality/accomplishment.

Q: What does the MBTI measure?

A: MBTI measures nothing more or less than your "preferred" way of responding to a variety of events. The definition of each of the four pairs of opposites is very precisely defined. One's MBTI "type" is simply an indicator of those preferences. It is not an excuse for anything, although many people use it that way. "Oh, I'm a P—I'm just naturally late"—that kind of stuff.

The folks at CPP that own the rights to the instrument have tried their darnedest to make sure only certified practitioners administer and assess the MBTI, but they can't police everyone. The instrument, in my opinion, should never be used for hiring/firing or promotional decisions. It is, however, a great tool for understanding how your co-workers/peers, reporters, or bosses may respond to various situational constructs and how you may be inclined to as well.

Q: What are the personality tests for honesty being used by many corporations?

A: There are a variety of "honesty" instruments, from AcuTrak to the Reid Interview. Reid is a cool technique.

Q: Can one learn to "game" a test?

A: What is the point of learning to "game" a test if you wind up in the wrong job? I, for example, am stupendous at taking all kinds of tests, because most are multiple guess and I can infer the answer from the question. But I guarantee you that you wouldn't want me performing cardiovascular surgery on you, irrespective of what my specialty practice results show on paper.

Q: Can the MBTI tell you where the "areas of stress most likely occur?"

A: MBTI is great for this. For example, when I get overstressed, I retreat into my non-dominant preferences—like the J-P preference. Normally a "come to closure type as a J," I *don't* or won't make decisions. I procrastinate—which to a J, of course, just heightens my stress.

I am an INTJ, and my N preference (intuition) is off the charts. But because I am introverted, my most defined attribute, intuition—the N preference—doesn't "show" itself publicly. People get my logic-based, fact-based, closure-based "let's move like we have a purpose here, people" self.

But if people start digging into how I came up with an idea, I can't tell them in a structured, linear, measurable way, which makes S (sensor) types very nervous. They just don't trust it. I once ran the education and programs function of engineering and surveying trade association, and as a group we went through MBTI. It was this experience that made me decide to get certified.

Everyone in my office was an ISTJ. I was an INTJ. And our long-suffering receptionist was an ENFP, a friendly, chatty, easygoing older lady who suffered terribly at the fact that none of us saw the need or had any interest in emotional bonding or water-cooler socializing. And we all vanished into our offices and worked quietly all day. Thank God she had the phones and visitor traffic for some human interface.

My N in an office of S's only was a problem when I was doing the creative part of my work. Then my ideas came out of nowhere and everywhere, without "evidence" to support them. And I (to them) often sounded conversationally unfocused. To me that's just the "normal" keeping of 17 conversational topics and/or possibilities aloft. I know where I am, why don't you?

I think the above example is great for showing what MBTI should be utilized for: understanding people's basic inclinations, what "feeds" them at work, what might not, and how to draw on each other's strengths and mitigate the less than optimal.

We all made an effort to be more "sociable" with the receptionist after we did our group session. And she really appreciated it, which, of course, made all of us (working against our innate preferences) feel good about our "stretching" for the benefit of our office mate.

Q: What tests do you give?

A: I am a certified MBTI practitioner (1995 from Type Resources) and am a three time national award winner for excellence in corporate training and development. I've been in my field for two-plus decades. I did my advanced studies in education and instructional design, which included psychometrics, testing, and instrumentation design. (But I didn't finish my Master's, truth in advertising).

Q: What works and what doesn't work in the way of tests?

A: Many of us are terrible at timed tests (except me). I'm the kid always turning to the next page before told to do so, which makes me show up as a "rule violator" on most assessments. And you can quote that!

So the best thing you can do is what everyone always says about test taking: *Relax.* Don't read too much into any one question. And your first answer impulse is the best answer/impulse, especially in the "no right/wrong" world or "personality" assessments. *Be yourself*, because someone has to, and you're the closest. Smile.

Some of the goals of corporate testing are to reduce risk, time, and expense. Employers use the test results to assess these as they relate to human resources. Abilities tests quantify job skills. They are also used to measure cognitive intelligence, intellectual reasoning abilities, and what is commonly known as "critical thinking." Abilities tests are often given along with personality profiles. Although personality tests are not supposed to be used for hiring decisions, in reality, some employers do use them for that purpose.

Chapter 7

Understanding Personality Profile Testing

Do you see yourself as average, normal, and outgoing? Or has your history revealed to you that you're a loner, introverted, creative, or reflective, or that you fit any other description? What's your profile? Make a list of 20 ways that you see yourself.

Ask a person who spends a lot of time with you to list 20 ways that show how that person perceives you as far as personality traits. Then make a list representing any differences between how you see yourself and how others perceive you. Here's how the lists might look:

Your List

1. Introverted/Reflective.
2. Loner/Love solitary environments outdoors/nature.
3. Reclusive.
4. Shy, few friends.
5. Sentimental.
6. Average-looking, short, thin.
7. Don't enjoy surprises/causes panic.
8. Average intelligence.
9. Independent/Entrepreneurial.
10. Musical.
11. Imaginative/Visionary/Creative.
12. Celebrate life.
13. Religious/Fervent.
14. Tire easily/Need constant change.
15. Enjoy working at home online.
16. Afternoon person/tired in mornings.
17. Empathic.
18. Sensitive/Doesn't like to be touched.
19. Unable to take much criticism at work unless it's about improving nutrition.
20. Slow to make decisions.

Your Relative's/Friend's Perception

1. Extroverted/Outgoing.
2. Expressive.
3. Energetic.
4. Religious/Fervor.
5. Party Person.
6. Excellent public speaker.
7. Above-average intelligence.
8. Creative.
9. Imaginative.
10. Attractive.
11. Nurturing.
12. Family-oriented.
13. Able to make quick decisions.
14. Very organized.
15. Objective.
16. Rational.
17. Inventive.
18. Decisive.
19. Traditional.
20. History buff/relies on polls and public opinions to make decisions.

As you can see, how someone else perceives your personality may be opposite or different from how you see yourself, or comparative lists made by several of your close relatives or friends may be similar. There may be a huge gap between how you see yourself and how others see you.

Personality profiles try to narrow that gap between what you'd like to be and what you are. How people see you could be how you'd like to be seen or how you come across. The way you see (or rate) yourself could agree or disagree in any way with how others see you.

It all depends upon what questions are asked on a personality profile. Abilities tests looking for critical-thinking skills or cognitive intelligence measure different types of capabilities. But a personality profile might be how you see yourself on a certain day and may change a week later.

Finding the real you—the consistent you—means looking at how you act under stress. Your "real" personality comes out when you're under stress and can no longer wear the mask under pressure of how you want to be or how you want others to see you. Test publishers tell employers that the purpose of testing at all levels of employment is to identify satisfying work for which you are well-suited.

Avoiding Exaggeration When Testing

Test designers usually recommend that you don't exaggerate your personality characteristics, values, or abilities. Questionnaires are supposed to give a fair and balanced assessment of how you match a variety of jobs. Personality assessments given at work are supposed to reveal *typical* corporate-related attitudes and values. The purpose of a corporate test is to see how well you are suited to the tasks and duties of a particular job.

You're supposed to see yourself taking a corporate test to identify further training and job development requirements needed. You're taking tests to understand what resources you use for motivation.

Personality tests usually are given along with abilities tests and decision-making assessments. The focus is on leadership training. Skill testing also screens out job applicants.

When constructing your own tests, the hard part is refining the questions and answers so you could separate the winners from the wash-outs in stockbroker training schools. Harder still would be validating the test's predictions by giving the test to students studying to become stock brokers.

You'd have to see whether their scores predict that the students will successfully find and stay in jobs such as stockbroker/registered representative jobs. Instead of developing your own tests to prepare to take a corporate test, focus on the short cut. Buy some practice tests from the test publisher who supplies your boss.

Corporate test sales, reputation, and income depend upon determining the predictive validity of their tests. Read the reviews of the tests in your local or university library and online.

Are the items on the abilities or personality tests your boss gives you relevant to your job performance? If you score low on math or spatial relations on an intelligence test, how would that relate to your job performance as an editor or newspaper reporter, where it's important to score high on verbal abilities?

It's possible that the coach read one interpretation of that test or heard a presentation at a conference that might differ from another interpretation the coach overlooked. Information overload plays a role. Assessments change. Tests are adapted. Variation on themes is common.

Managers have been warned not to hire or fire by personality or intelligence assessment results. But sometimes they do. Most profoundly, managers don't hire those who score high on tests of anger measurement.

What Organizational and Social Psychologists Say

What licensed organizational and social psychologists say about how you might see yourself on corporate tests may be similar or different from what career, executive, and life coaches say regarding how you could see yourself. Trainers, consultants, counselors, educational technologists, psychometrists, psychologists, human resource managers, and corporate testing/scoring software designers look at your assessment results in perspective from their varied backgrounds.

Most organizational psychologists agree that the majority of corporations are not *consistent* in the types of tests they administer. However, when career coaches are contacted at random, almost all of them are familiar with the most popular personality type and/or job task preference assessments.

Corporations may choose to contract organizational psychologists or career coaches. An organizational psychologist generally has a doctorate degree in organizational or social psychology. A career coach may come from a wide, interdisciplinary background with varying educational certifications.

Usually career coaches don't design individual tests for specific clients. They usually offer tests that already are published with the major test publishers. Organizational psychologists may design their own tests in certain cases. It all depends upon what corporation leaders require of a human resources or competency management company. Usually, what a corporation and its clients want in the way of corporate tests is validation and monitoring.

Maximizing Human Resources With Testing

Meet social-industrial psychologist, Jeffrey W. Daum, Ph.D. Dr. Daum is CEO of Competency Management Incorporated (CMI). A footnote on CMI's stationery reads: "Realizing Excellence Through Human Resources."

Dr. Daum has been engaged in the practical application of behavioral science to business and organizations for more than 30 years. As a consultant his emphasis has been on designing and implementing programs that endeavor to maximize the human resource side of running an organization. This includes focusing on competency-based recruiting, interviewing, testing, selection, promotion, and assessment.

Competency Management Incorporated (CMI) has a division that designs, validates, implements and monitors testing programs for corporations and organizations. The corporation tailors these tests for each client (with a few exceptions, where it identifies an existing test that meets the client's needs) to ensure a good match on several important elements including the client's culture and objectives.

Dr. Jeffrey W. Daum answered Anne's following e-mail interview questions for this book on July 17, 2006:

Q: How do you advise your clients to take any specific corporate test?

A: We do not normally find ourselves advising clients how to take any specific corporate test. For some of our client's applications, we do design an introduction to potential test takers to explain what they can expect as to content covered, style of questions. However, this is very specific to the test battery that we develop for that client. The best *generic* advice I can provide to individuals that are going to take a test, whether they are being considered for joining an organization or as part of a possible promotion, is to be truthful and honest. No matter what the specific test is designed for, the penultimate objective (of a professionally developed test) is to ensure the best match with the essential job requirements.

If an individual attempts to fake the test (or interview, considered under Federal law the same as a test, or job simulation, or assessment center exercises) or give what he or she thinks are socially appropriate responses but not really reflecting his own in the hopes of getting into the organization or gaining the promotion, the odds are he will find himself either in a job he does not like, or in a job he cannot handle, or failing the test because he "tripped" the lie scale built into many assessments.

Q: What do corporate tests measure most frequently at which levels?

A: There really is not a clear answer to this question because of the vast range of differences across corporations globally and within their testing programs. It should be driven by what the job analysis indicates are the essential competencies. CMI's operational definition of essential competencies is "those skills, abilities, knowledge and personality characteristics that are necessary to successfully complete the job."

So the test will vary based on the jobs the organization is looking to fill. As you would expect, the level and complexity of the job requirements (should) result in very different testing requirements.

In the United States, Fair Employment Legislation prohibits an organization from arbitrarily testing for non-job related competencies if the tests will have adverse impact on a protected class individual—that is, if the test will prevent a person from being considered for a job that he or she actually could handle because of poorer performance on any non-job related competency.

For example, if the person is applying for a job that does not use basic math skills, yet the battery he has to take for the job includes basic math skills and as a result screens out a higher portion of protected class individuals, the test battery would be considered illegal.

Q: What kind of corporate tests are given other than personality profile or cognitive abilities tests?

A: Today there are both legitimate professionally developed and validated tests and non-professionally developed non-validated tests across the corporate environment that assess just about everything and have blurred the categories of personality profiles or cognitive ability tests. *Bio-inventory tests* have become quite popular, and they are a variation on personality profiling tests.

Job simulation tests replicate everything from how to repair and paint a wall to how to be a team leader or manager. Work ethic tests are derived from a similar approach to designing a behaviorally based interview combined with situational tests.

Culture-free tests (designed to get around language dependency and the impact of formal education) that are typically based on images or measuring neural impulses have gone in and out of fashion over the past few decades.

Q: Are job skills tests more popular than the personality surveys?

A: There are times when only job skill tests are appropriate, and times when personality tests are appropriate, and times when a combined battery would be appropriate including both types. Personality tests have come under greater court scrutiny in the last decade than skill tests, particularly concerning invasion-of-privacy laws that many states have.

I would guess that across all industries, if you were looking at how many *professionally developed and validated tests* of either skill or personality were used, you would find more skill tests used. Some specific industries, such as public protection and sales have a higher reliance on personality-based instruments.

Q: Are intelligence tests given to job applicants for entry-level clerical workers and executives alike?

A: I would hope not. Pure intelligence tests, like personality tests, have appropriately come under greater court scrutiny since the coming of civil rights legislation. Most organizations would have a hard time justifying any pure intelligence test for entry-level positions.

Clerical workers normally would be tested based on a job analysis on attention to detail, specific language competency in both oral and written communication, sorting skills, and, if appropriate, word-processing skills. For the executive, you should be looking for assessment of job related competencies that you do not already have comparable information on based on the individual's known work history.

Q: Are most personality assessments given at the same time with other tests, such as test of abilities or decision making skills?

A: Again, this would be dependent on the specific objectives of the client and how the individual's testing program is set up. Often, a test battery is designed to give the most cost efficient test first to winnow down the potential candidates, and then the more expensive tests to the remaining candidates. So some organizations do it over a period of time or sessions, whereas others may put everyone through the entire battery at one sitting.

Q: Are corporate tests given for one main purpose, such as building better teams?

A: There really is not a single "corporate test" or single reason that corporations test. There is not a high consistency on what corporations actually test. Certainly some organizations use assessments to identify the best composition of team members, or to improve team effectiveness. However, as detailed in the links referenced on our Website, there are many different reasons to assess individuals.

[More detail on CMI's tests can be found at *www.cmihr.com/testing.shtml*, *www.cmihr.com/work.shtml*, *competencymanagement.com/preemp.shtml*, and elsewhere on CMI's public Website (*www.cmihr.com*).]

Q: **How do you minimize the potential for adverse impact and maximize the best match?**

A: The results of our job analysis include minimizing or eliminating the potential for adverse impact while maximizing the best match from potential candidates. The short answer to this is that you design the test to be highly job related and assess essential competencies required the first day on the job as compared to being necessary at some future point in the job or the person's career.

The type/style of questions, the required response format and overall type of assessment are carefully considered and developed to minimize potential for adverse impact. Carefully constructed validation of the outcome of test and, if appropriate, each test item of the test is further designed to identify any potential problem areas. If found, these are refined if possible prior to the actual roll out and use of the test in the client's setting.

3M's Talent Management Corporate Testing

Discover Your Personality.com (*www.discoveryourpersonality.com/ clients.html*) has a list naming major corporations that use corporate testing, including personality assessments. Anne chose at random one corporation to contact—3M—and invited its human resources division (Talent Management) to answer the question, "Why test applicants?"

In her reply of July 11, 2006, Karen B. Paul, Ph.D, of 3M Center's Talent Management, in St. Paul, Minnesota, said:

> 3M has a long tradition of pre-employment testing for certain job groupings. Testing leads to savings in the decision-making process. Employment tests can be a cost-effective way to pare down the applicant pool. Tests can make the decision process more efficient because less time is spent with individuals whose characteristics, skills, and abilities do not match what is needed to do the job well.
>
> The costs of making a wrong decision are high. For certain employment decisions, a wrong decision can be very costly in terms of training costs, errors made by a poor performer, costs of replacement, etc. For these types of decisions, investing in testing is particularly worthwhile endeavor if testing reduces the number of wrong decisions.
>
> Testing for fit with the organization can result in higher retention. Tests can produce savings through not training and compensating individuals whose productivity would be low or who would not remain on the job.
>
> Hard-to-get information can be obtained more easily and efficiently. One important advantage of using pre-hire tests is that they can often provide information about an individual that is not

easily obtained using other methods, or that would be much more costly to obtain by other means.

Individuals are treated consistently. Using standardized tools in employment decision-making ensures that the same information is gathered on each individual and used in a similar way in decisions.

There are a lot of applicants. Sometimes the sheer number of individuals to consider for an employment decision leads an employer to choose testing as the most efficient and fair means of making a decision quickly.

3M's Talent Management division also referred Anne to the Society of Industrial and Organizational Psychology Website (*www.siop.org/*) for a full exploration of the topic.

Creating the Tests

Theoretically, any employer can hire anyone with experience in designing computer-scored corporate tests with expert knowledge of the specific job skills tested. Most of the commercially published corporate tests used by major companies are designed by industrial and organizational psychologists. If you have no degree and are a self-motivated learner, there's always some type of test you could design and market to corporate clients, tutors, or others in your special field of expertise or experience. Test designers usually call on past experience and knowledge when designing tests. As a test-taker, it is a challenge to guess what the test designer knew or used when designing the test you are taking.

Those organizational/industrial psychologists who design corporate tests for major test publishers first conduct research in order to understand and measure human behavior. Corporate tests are designed in order to improve employees' workplace satisfaction.

Corporate tests are bought by the employer, not by the employee. What the employer looks for in a corporate test is its ability to help the employer choose or promote the best qualified people. Employers believe testing leads to overall improvement.

The goal of corporate testing for psychologists who design tests is to improve workplace social environments for employees because workers far outnumber employers. The end result for the employer would be increased production, less turnover, and more income.

Industrial psychologists create tests and design training courses. They write procedures for employee selection and create surveys. They can be outsourced, brought in as independent contractors, or employed as part of the HR department of a corporation.

Industrial and organizational psychologists may work only for test publishing companies that produce widely published test instruments purchased by the human resources or educational technology/marketing departments of corporations. Or they can work independently as coaches.

Industrial and organizational psychologists usually direct consulting and executive search firms. They open leadership centers. Some run their own corporations or work as consultants. Organizational psychologists also teach and do research for universities and think tanks.

What mostly all organizational psychologists do is research how work forces are managed in order to provide information to corporations or to create studies or tests. The content of studies, surveys, and assessments could be anything from what stigmas arise in organizations to how personality plays a role in the hiring process.

Organizational psychologists study harassment, ageism, disability, orientation, honesty, theft, attractiveness, beliefs, aggression, downsizing, and a wide variety of barriers or boons to successful workplace culture. They study discrimination and preference at work. Organizational psychologists also study what happens when companies merge. They are active in designing tests for or studying how law enforcement officers are selected. These types of psychologists also research ways to cut down on absenteeism.

In addition to the usual tests, organizational psychologists create tests and surveys to find out what attracts job applicants to specific companies. They create tests to measure and study various aspects of leadership behavior differences between male and female managers. Corporate testing is more than a personality profile, job skills assessment, or IQ test.

Organizational Communications Management

Another related field in which corporations may test you is how you share meaning. It's called organizational communications management. Testing examines aspects of communications—how management and workers use downward, upward, body, verbal, written, formal, informal, interpersonal and group communication. This type of testing could be used with team-building groups or along with tests of decision-making ability.

Organizational communication is the study of how people communicate inside an organization and how the organization influences interaction between employees and employers. Tests are designed to find out differences between how workers share meaning with one another and how they communicate with management.

Problems in workplace communication are researched and surveyed by some corporate tests that emphasize how employees effectively convey and receive information. The goal of testing is to analyze the problems testing reveals. Then those problems may be solved by applying different efforts at internal and external corporate communications.

Managers believe effective communications is the foundation for effectiveness in any area of organization. Too many office memos are full of miscommunications because meaning isn't shared consistently or is interpreted differently by various departments that don't interact frequently.

The goal in exploring organizational psychology or communications management is to find out how the tests you take are designed because the results may be stored in your permanent records. For further information, contact the Association for Business Communication (*www.businesscommunication.org/*).

？ ？ ？ ？ ？ ？ ？ ？

Chapter 8

Why Employers Use
Testing

Some decision-making abilities tests are based upon entertaining simulation games that show how each person's decision can influence changes that affect the future, including survival. One decision-making ability test simulation is a scenario tool in use around the world called Quest. First tried in Vancouver, the decision-making simulation software uses visual aides to show various aspects of different trends.

It was said at one presentation of Quest's software that decisions influence sustainability. Quest uses a simulation to test decision-making using a score based upon nine trends of sustainability—including unemployment and ecology. Decision-making abilities tests are tools for corporate survival.

Employers test your decision-making ability to ensure that the long-term implications of their decisions don't fall through the cracks due to your "daily demands." Employers want to make sure that "plans and visions" aren't swept away in the rush because you overlooked information.

Among the wide variety of corporate tests for decision-making ability, a simulation might be placed in front of you. The decision-making test could be inter-active software, paper multiple-choice questions, or three-dimensional models that simulate corporate projects. You're asked to observe the details and decide.

You're timed, perhaps one minute, per decision. Did you miss any important details in your haste to decide? Your team or trainer may point out the blind spots derailing your decision. If you're a pilot, you make decisions while training on a flight simulator. In numerous decision-making assessments, you're in an interactive seminar.

A test of decision-making ability might use software (or paper) that gives you five or six choices. If you're only given one minute to make a decision, you may be asked to choose one selection from five or six multiple answers for each question based on a scale. You'd have to indicate a number for each answer by checking one answer as your *first* choice.

Your decision is judged as good or bad by a *vote* from your team and/or employer. The group that benefits most from decision-making training and testing ultimately is the community affected by the long-term outcome of corporate or government decisions.

Decision Focus is another popular software module for training, published by Focus Performance Systems. The modules train you to more effectively solve problems, make decisions, and execute plans faster. Decision Focus products are described online (*www.focustools.com//prodserv.cfm/PSNav/dec_focus*).

Good Decisions vs. Bad Decisions

A bad decision occurs when vital details are overlooked. A good decision happens when insight, hindsight, foresight, and research uncover hidden information that shows step by step how to avoid pitfalls, solve problems, and get results. Testing can reveal if your boss gives you enough time to make good decisions. Training shows you how to prioritize, organize, and multi-task.

Do decision-making assessments reward executives with creativity enhancement kudos for breaking certain company rules to improve services? And do employers punish entry-level job-applicants that indicate on corporate tests they don't strongly agree with strictly obeying company rules in every instance imaginable?

Employers perceive the "working poor" differently than they view executives. You can see the emphasis on strict obedience to company rules in the corporate tests given to low-wage job applicants.

It's necessary for safety, say employers. But what happens when there's an exception to a rule that the company wants you to obey at all times? Breaking a rule means making a decision. The decision may be evaluated as "good" or "bad" based on whether it improves the corporation.

Making good or bad decisions is emphasized on corporate tests taken by managers. Evaluations are about rhetoric. Corporate testing of low-level employees is primarily focused on making sure the employee obeys company rules.

Corporations need to be sure that under steady decreases in time and staff that your managerial decisions remain sound. A good decision leads to improvement in your company's profit, image, and employee-retention rate. A bad decision is expensive.

Executives and other company leaders are evaluated on how good their decisions are, with training offered to improve too many 'bad' decisions. Leadership training is tailored to improve methods used to arrive at 'good' (organized, tested) decisions.

Employers who test the entire staff are interested in the decisions of high- and low-level employees in different ways. Depending upon status and salary in the company, you're given different types of personality assessments.

Interestingly, companies that experience the highest rates of annual employee turnover of low-level workers may frequently give low-level employees multiple-choice personality assessments that focus on questions about obedience and honesty. A century ago, servants would have been asked similar questions about honesty and following rules strictly.

With low-level workers, strict obedience is wanted regarding company rules. Some retail customer service employees see the corporation as an extension of a manor house requiring "service with a smile."

Testing usually is not seen as an open door leading to promotion to retail buyer, decorator, or manager. Factory workers may view corporate testing as a chance for promotion to supervisor or further training in a specialty technology such as robotics or computer operation.

With low-level employees, strong agreement to questions about following company rules defines a "good" decision. The test-taker has no way to make a managerial-type "good decision" by disobeying company rules when a rare exception to a rule appears.

The tests, often timed and scored by computers, are interpreted usually by one manager who decides whether to hire the job applicant. The decision to hire may be based on how strongly the job applicant agrees with company rules.

Do some employees taking timed tests actually look for rare exceptions as reasons to disagree with and challenge test questions? That depends upon whether the employee is trying to distinguish possible safety issues occurring in the workplace. The key is not to make a test of agreement with company rules complicated.

Don't let your "what if" concepts leap ahead of basic, simple logic. Tests of decision-making often boil down to a list of pros and cons. You go with the longer list.

Corporate test taking experiences at various levels have been widely publicized in the media. A fascinating personal experience regarding corporate testing of entry level, low-paid job applicants appears in Chapter 3 of Barbara Ehrenreich's 2001 book, *Nickel and Dimed*.

Tests are interpreted for the employer. The best 'score' at some companies could be hired rather than the whole person, so to speak. Companies reflect the decisions, values, and attitudes of their leaders. Your goal is to match your values or outlook to those of a corporation's leaders. Consider also a company's philosophy, plans, and goals.

The Built-In Lie Scale Alarm in Corporate Anger Assessments

Popular tests on the market with built-in lie scale alarms are supposed to reveal anger levels or disruptive behavior. If you repeatedly say that you *strongly agree* with a list of sentences that report behaviors that most people don't do, the built-in lie scale alarm will be set off.

Even if the correct answer is that you disagree somewhat, your answer needs to be somewhere in the middle. Your answer needs to show common sense. Most people will answer such statements honestly and not use superlatives or strongly agree with all-encompassing generalities such as "I have never lost a friend."

If you strongly agree, the lie scale would be tripped. It's assumed that somewhere in your lifetime between age 2 and the present you lost contact with a friend. So watch those sentences with words such as *never* or *always*.

For example, on an anger test of statements, there might be a sentence that reads, "I've never said any words that hurt someone's feelings." If you check a box that says "I strongly agree," then the lie scale will be tripped.

Your sensibilities tell you that some time in your childhood you used words to a classmate, parent, sibling, or stranger that may have hurt his or her feelings. Anger test statements are put there to set off lie alarms if you strongly agree with a negative or "never" statement or strongly agree with a positive or "always" statement as in "I always found the perfect boss and the perfect job each time I applied." That's why you need to select moderate, sensible, middle-of-the-road or neutral categories such as "I somewhat agree" or "I somewhat disagree."

The "strongly disagree" or "strongly agree" answers trip the lie scale alarm on tests of anger and sometimes on tests of honesty. However, in the case of honesty tests, a corporation's insistence that you show total loyalty to the company usually emphasizes that you check the box that says "I strongly agree" about reporting customer theft or co-worker theft, safety issues, or breaking of rules by fellow workers. Corporations would want you to report rule-breaking co-worker behavior such as smoking marijuana or taking street drugs at work, destroying property, theft, or any other unsafe behavior at work.

Anger assessments designed to screen out angry, disruptive behavior usually are given to job applicants, but may also be given to employees who are reported to be disruptive. Angry people could potentially be disruptive in the workplace. There's always the chance of violent behavior or road rage leading to disaster.

Interviewers may be warned not to hire people so filled with rage that a potential for violence in the workplace or on the road commuting to or from work might happen. Troubled employees or applicants who have turned anger inwards could reach a stage where the anger is finally turned out and directed to employers, co-workers, or relatives.

Stress tests also may be given. It's difficult for employers and interviewers to generalize about people from first appearance or words taken out of context. That's why a battery of tests might be given.

Screening Angry, Disruptive Individuals at Work

Managers don't want you to visibly show anger at work. They want you to create alternatives—such as doing crossword puzzles while waiting your turn or for an event to begin. At work, it may be stopping work on one assigned task, and returning to another. For example, stop working on a problematic claim file, and instead work on a different case.

On a corporate test that uses scales to measure anger, you're not supposed to loudly express impatience on a long line, when a car cuts in front of you, or while waiting for a speaker who arrives a half hour late. You're supposed to remain calm or innovative enough to start a conversation, use earphones, or read while cooling your heels. Calmness and distraction is the emotionally mature choice.

There could be 100 or more statements on an anger test, or there could be only a few statements, depending upon the various tests. Such tests may be timed or untimed.

Employers know that really angry people would probably try to cover up emotions during a job interview and present the calmest face or 'mask.' That's why anger tests have built-in lie scale alarms.

Some corporate human resource divisions are familiar with research studies that report when a person's heart rate/pulse rate and blood pressure go down when the individual is very angry, that may be a warning sign of possible future disruptive behavior. A normal person's anxiety level would cause the heart rate and blood pressure to go up/increase when angry or under stress.

The underaroused central nervous system during or after an angry outburst is to be watched, say some books. This does not mean that a person who keeps his or her cool and stays calm in a crisis has a problem. It only means to watch a person who loudly and volcanically explodes in anger, but whose pulse and blood pressure goes down during and immediately after the loud explosive behavior. The angry, disruptive co-worker may have an under-aroused central nervous system that needs stimulation in ways that are not appropriate, or the individual could be intermittently explosive for inappropriate reasons.

That's what some assessments are designed to bring to the notice of employers, test scorers, and interviewers. Nowadays, many tests are taken online and scored by computers. It may be a long time before an anger test is brought to a supervisor's attention.

It is generally thought that one in 10 people in the U.S. population has some form of a mental illness. So managers are on guard for angry, depressed, disruptive, and potentially violent. The sample test that follows is designed to detect anger or potential for disruptive behavior. Simple tests, such as the sample in Appendix C, are designed to detect the potential for disruptive behavior.

Determining Emotional Maturity Testing

Managers don't want to hear about bullies or co-workers who irritate you or get on your nerves, or how you got even. Anger measurement multiple-choice questions are imbedded in many personality assessments. Numerous tests are designed to screen you out.

The human resources department of a corporation is the place appointed to screen out people. The public relations department of a corporation is the place where people are invited in to observe.

To avoid barriers to screen you out, you need to present your skills directly to the head of the department where you want to work. Ask for an internship if you have no experience.

Managers also have been warned not to hire or fire based on advanced age, but they also do. Scales are made for measuring emotions. And hiring is done by looking at scales, such as how slow you are to anger.

Find out what mature attitudes the most desirable candidate should possess. Personality tests look for emotional maturity. With your personality and abilities, would you really be happy in that job working for and representing that company and its managers?

Do you want to be a poster picture standing in for that company? Do your values match that corporation's values?

Are you happy imitating successful giants, being part of a big institution, and following tradition? Or would you prefer to seek rapid change by looking into your future? Are you happier being more imaginative and visionary than repetitive and routine?

What responsibility scares you the most? Would you rate yourself "definitely hire?" Or would you be better off running your own show?

If you were your boss, would you hire someone with your abilities and attitudes? You're presenting to the public an image of your boss's corporation.

The best way to take a corporate test is by learning what management wants. Ethically, you're supposed to give honest answers.

If you're honest, which you should be, you may not get the job because your prospective employer may want a certain "personality type." Perhaps an interviewer has been told by a coach that a specific personality label is better suited for the job.

Why Some Employers Select by Personality Preferences

Most personality assessments assign you to an aspect of personality such as a preference, trait, style, or type. Personality questionnaires may be called classifiers, indicators, or assessments.

You'll be classified according to *aspects* of your personality that you possess to a greater or lesser degree because executives require a system to label, measure, and classify you according to your character traits. You're classified according to your choices or attitudes.

Being classified is one way to measure you. There are no wrong answers. You're not "graded" on a personality assessment. Personality assessments look for predictable differences.

Numerous personality assessments are based on the research and theories of Swiss psychoanalyst Carl Jung. Personality assessments are about preferences—based on the way we prefer and choose to take in information, decide, explore, and express ourselves.

Some personality assessments label us according to our temperaments or types, and other classifiers show us our traits, attitudes, or personality styles. What they all have in common is that they show us—give us a label for—the ways in which we prefer to behave.

Assessments reveal to us with a word, category, or label how we prefer to make decisions. Personality questionnaires explain in a word how we look at information and how we give directions.

Employers promote patient people with certain "sensible" or "creative" personality polarities—depending upon the job description. Most employers want someone who fits into the group. Corporations prefer to retain those who are slow to anger and quick to make decisions.

Suppose a manager needed to hire a traveling public speaker to connect charismatically with people for a permanent full-time job. Duties would be to teach leadership skills to executives and answer endless questions face to face with audiences. Would a person who consistently turns feelings inward or outward be selected for the job?

So you take a corporate personality assessment based on "being hired to do what you think you are" on that particular day. Or you take an assessment so many times at schools and career centers that you become familiar with which questions designate the various preferences.

Your personal styles are compared with the personal styles of others in similar careers. If you don't know yourself, or fear that, if you're honest, you won't be hired, you might select a different answer on another day. Sometimes you select an answer because you think the boss wants someone with that trait. You may answer differently each time you take a personality test. Some days you may feel more outgoing and energized. Another day you may feel more logical than sentimental.

111

If you take enough assessments or make a list of how you feel over a longer period of time about how you make decisions, you'll soon realize how you really act under stress. Do you make decisions by creating a logical list of pros and cons? Or do you make choices by your personal likes and dislikes—by sentiment, impulse, or daydreams? Do you tell yourself to forget how you feel emotionally and look rationally at your behavior? Or do you listen to your gut feelings?

Do you put the safety, behavior, and health of your children above your need to have someone you find controlling remain in the home mainly to financially support you? That list of pros and cons is a rational list, you hope, and you weigh the pros against the cons and decide to go with the longer list.

Personality assessments *in general* aren't supposed to tell you how to act, what to decide, or whether to hire. Don't use them to choose a job or a mate. They only point to aspects of your personality. Most personality assessments classify you according to your interests, or they take an inventory of your interests, preferences, and choices.

Some assessments are helpful if you want to see whether you'd be strongly motivated to run your own business for the long term under certain conditions, if you do enough marketing research and have the fortitude that entrepreneurship takes.

Read Allen L. Hammer's 2001 "Strong and MBTI® Entrepreneur Report" (*www.cpp.com/images/reports/smp289170.pdf*). The report for an individual (posted on the Web) on personality and entrepreneurship notes: "To help you determine whether running your own business is a good fit with your interests and personality, the information that follows is based on your results on the Strong Interest Inventory™ (Strong) and Myers-Briggs Type Indicator® (MBTI®) inventory."

Personality tests point out potential leaders by evaluating values, attitudes, expectations, decision-making, or motivations. Perhaps a test points out people who adapt easily to frequent flying, overseas travel, night work, or numerical ability. Maybe the criterion of the test is to search for executives who make consistently good decisions, or to fill a new job opening in management.

The criterion of a test might be to see how well you connect with co-workers, show empathy, objectivity, and emotional maturity. Is it an assessment of social smarts, personality, or cognitive intelligence? Are the test results statistically significant? How has the test been compared with large groups of test-takers?

Reading test reviews helps when you know little about corporate tests. Most personality traits are experienced in varying degrees by most people. Appendix D features Anne's sample 74-question Interests-in-Common Classifier. Your answers reveal your either-or choice. It's a preference classifier that shows you what you like to do—some of your interests. Use it to make a list of pros and cons. Such a list can give you clues. That's what you're looking for in this type of assessment: clues to what you'd prefer, or what the best-fit situation is for you.

Clues motivate you to search for evidence. Facts and history are evidence. In what direction do the clues point?

There are no wrong answers. When you add up your choices, you'll get a mini-picture of what works for you. The assessment is designed to see what you have in common with others who have similar preferences, choices, or interests.

Why Employers Use the Testing

The greatest challenge for employers is placing the right people in the right jobs. To find out which are the right people for specific jobs, employers use personality, abilities, and skills testing. The most timorous answer within the testing industry is to find the current but ever-changing reply when employers ask the necessary question, "What does testing cost employers?" You can't say a pretty penny any longer. Instead, you can have employers take and sample simulations of various preference and personality classifiers before they give those assessments to their workers. (To see how well grounded you are, try the High-Tech/Low Tech Career and Personality Preference Classifier in Appendix E.)

Conclusion

What all employment personality assessments have in common is that they specify a number of traits, such as descriptions based on Jungian theories and writings. Some tests have proven themselves statistically, and are translated in many languages and used successfully in various countries, and some assessments work only part of the time because the test-taker may not know what he or she really prefers. Most employment personality assessments are not tests, but questionnaires, classifiers, and various indicators that rely on the test taker being truthful about his or her personality. Your personality is what comes to the surface when you are under a lot of stress and the "real you" emerges. At that time you'll know whether you are outgoing under stress, for example, or prefer to be alone. You'll know whether you want to listen to theories and ideas, look for patterns in nature, or learn some practical skills related to your job.

Under stress, you'll realize what you are about. You'll learn to know yourself more. That's why it's important to make a list of these clues to your own personality. To find yourself, look for descriptions of your own behavior at work under stress in your dictionary and thesaurus. That's the origin for what's on most of these personality assessments given at work, whether organizational psychologists score them or you score them yourself.

Each assessment may use a different word to describe or define a separate personality trait useful on employment assessments. For example, some tests use words familiar to readers of C. G. Jung's writings on eight personality traits. Other tests rely on terms defining good decision-making abilities. Some tests rely on peer evaluation, whereas other tests are sent away to professional psychometric scoring services at the various test publishers' companies to be scored. Still others are self-scoring and offer immediate results and interpretations.

No matter what the specifics are for a particular assessment, pay close attention, as it will give you insight into who you really are.

? ? ? ? ? ? ? ?

Appendix A

The "King Toot" Creative Writing Aptitude Classifier

Are you best suited to be a digital interactive storywriter on ancient Egypt, a nonfiction writer, or a mystery writer using ancient Egyptian themes or related ancient themes? Do you think the way a fiction writer does? Take the writing style preference classifier and find out how you approach your favorite writing style using Toot's facts and acts.

Which genre is for you: interactive, traditional, creative nonfiction, fiction, decisive, or investigative? Would you rather write for readers that need to interact with their own story endings or plot branches? Which style best fits you? What's your writing profile?

Take this ancient echoes writing-genre interest classifier and see the various ways in which way you can be more creative. Do you prefer to write investigative, logical nonfiction or imaginative fiction—or a mixture of both? There are 35 questions—seven questions for each of the five pairs. The ten categories are made up of five pairs of opposites.

The Choices:

Grounded	↔	Verve
Rational	↔	Enthusiastic
Decisive	↔	Investigative
Loner	↔	Outgoing
Traditional	↔	Change-Driven

Writer's Creativity Style Classifier

You are a **mystery writer** working on an interactive audio book of stories with clues for the Web about a scribe in ancient Egypt, 1350 BC, who has unending adventures trying to track down the person who bashed King Toot with a golden vulture mallet and a cobra-headed hammer.

Your scribe is in a race against time to save Toot's teenaged widow, Ankh-Es-En-Amen, from being forced into an unwilling marriage with Toot's male nanny-Regent, Aye, who is determined to become Pharaoh by marrying the Queen. How will you write this interactive story, according to your writing style preferences?

Clues

The leading character is *Mose*, the scribe, not the prophet Moses. The name Mose or Moses in ancient Egyptian means "from the water." The name *Toot Mose* means "wise one from the water." (The name usually means "gift of the Nile.") *Toot* means wise and is represented in hieroglyphics as an owl.

Mose inherited wealth from an ancestral line of architects. He's an Egyptian male scribe, age 20, living in the royal palace. He grew up as Toot's friend. Called "Mu" for short, this character is your alter ego and takes on your own personality as he solves problems or crimes.

1. To write your story, would you prefer to:
   - ❑ a. go to the Hittite archives in order to have translated two letters sent by Toot's teenage widow to the Hittite king asking to send her a new husband? (*grounded*)
   - ❑ b. dig deeper and find out the connections between the two documents, reading fear between the lines and noting the reluctance Toot's widow expresses in being forced to marry her servant, the Regent Aye? (*verve*)

2. Would you be more interested in researching history and writing about:
   - ❑ a. the closeness of the relationship that surfaced between the Hittites and the Egyptians in 1350 BCE? (*enthusiastic*)
   - ❑ b. the analysis of the business deals and diplomatic events between these equal powers to see who was winning the race to becoming the superpower of the century? (*rational*)

3. Are you more interested in the fact that:
   - ❑ a. Toot's queen wrote all her letters in a Hittite dialect, not in Egyptian? (*grounded*)
   - ❑ b. King Toot's father, Akhenaten, was so hated after his death because he worshipped one deity, that his face was scratched off all his monuments and wall friezes? (*verve*)

4. Would you rather write about:
   - ❏ a. Toot being adopted, sent as a gift from Hatti during his Egyptian stepfather's "durbar" festival of his 12th year of reign? (*enthusiastic*)
   - ❏ b. the mystery of why Toot was buried with both the Hittite vulture on his head and an Egyptian cobra on his crown? (*rational*)

5. You are Toot's Queen. Would you rather:
   - ❏ a. exercise your right as a widow to claim Toot's unmarried Hittite brother, Prince Zennanza? (*enthusiastic*)
   - ❏ b. marry Toot's male nanny, because it's only right and fair to restore an Egyptian to Egypt's throne? (*rational*)

6. Toot's widow wrote to her father-in-law to send another of his sons to marry her. As a writer of her life story, would you rather:
   - ❏ a. create a laundry list of princes that she must interview and screen in a dating game? (*grounded*)
   - ❏ b. create a story where she rides 1,000 miles on a donkey to run away from her servant after he forces her to marry him and has magical adventures disguised as a 14-year-old boy studying philosophy and alchemy with Babylonian astrologers? (*verve*)

7. Are you more interested in :
   - ❏ a. ending your story with Aye marrying Toot's young widow, then taking Toot's adoptive grandmother, Queen Tiye, as a second wife, so that you have closure and an ending for your story? (*decisive*)
   - ❏ b. letting your story remain open for serialization, because Toot's widow is never heard from again after Aye marries her and then marries Queen Tiye, because the fate of Toot's widow after marrying Aye is not recorded in history? (*investigative*)

8. If you were Prince Zennanza, would you prefer to :
   - ❏ a. decide immediately to obey the Hittite king and leave your own country to marry the widowed Queen of Egypt because duty required it, knowing you'd probably be killed when you arrived by the same person who killed Toot? (*decisive*)
   - ❏ b. stall for time as long as possible, waiting for validated information to arrive regarding the diplomatic climate between Hittites and Egyptians? (*investigative*)

9. You are King Toot, Pharaoh of Egypt, a Hittite prince adopted in infancy as a gift from the Hittite king because the Egyptian queen had six daughters. Would you:
   - ❏ a. speak in the Indo-European Hittite language in front of your Hamitic-speaking Egyptian Regent, thereby possibly inflaming the patriotism in him? (*investigative*)

❑ b. plan and organize methodically to have a whole line of people close to you from your own country of origin (in what is now central Turkey) rather than from Egypt, in which you were raised? (*decisive*)

10. Would you rather write about the:
    ❑ a. terms of the treaty between Hatti and Egypt based on the facts provided by records? (*grounded*)
    ❑ b. theories set in motion when Aye marries Toot's widow, and, soon after, the widow disappears, and Aye marries Queen Tiye? (*verve*)

11. Do you like writing about:
    ❑ a. enigmas or puzzles set in motion by symbols on intimate funerary equipment in a mystery novel? (*rational*)
    ❑ b. why no other Egyptian royalty or deities after Toot's life span ever again were depicted with a vulture being friendly with a cobra? (*enthusiastic*)

12. A *tag line* shows the mood/emotion in the voice—how a character speaks or acts. Are you more interested in:
    ❑ a. compiling, counting, and indexing *citations* or *quotes* from how-to books for writers? (*grounded*)
    ❑ b. compiling *tag lines* that explain in fiction dialogue the specific behaviors or gestures (such as, "Yes, he replied timorously.")? (*verve*)

13. Would you rather write:
    ❑ a. dialogue? (*enthusiastic*)
    ❑ b. description? (*rational*)

14. To publicize your writing, would you rather:
    ❑ a. give spectacular presentations or shows without preparation or prior notice? (*investigative*)
    ❑ b. prepare a long time in advance to speak or perform? (*decisive*)

15. If you were Queen Ankh-Es-En-Amen, would you prefer to:
    ❑ a. receive warnings well in advance and without surprises that Aye is planning to get rid of you and marry Queen Tiye (adoptive grandmother of Toot), so you could conveniently disappear? (*decisive*)
    ❑ b. adapt to last-moment changes by never getting down to your last man or your last beer? (*investigative*)

16. As a scribe, artist, and poet in ancient Egypt would you:
    ❑ a. feel constrained by King Toot's time schedules and deadlines? (*investigative*)
    ❑ b. set realistic timetables and juggle priorities? (*decisive*)

120

17. As Toot's widow, do you feel bound to:
    - ❏ a. go with social custom, do the activities itemized on the social calendar, and marry your dead husband's unmarried brother because it's organized according to a plan? (*decisive*)
    - ❏ b. go with the flow of the relationship, deal with issues as they arise, and make no commitments or assumptions about what's the right thing to do because time changes plans? (*investigative*)

18. You're the Hittite King, Shup-Pilu-Liu-Mas, reading Toot's widow's desperate letter in your own country. Is your reply to the Egyptian queen more likely to be:
    - ❏ a. a brief, concise, and to-the-point letter? (*rational*)
    - ❏ b. a sociable, friendly, empathetic, and time-consuming letter? (*enthusiastic*)

19. You're King Toot contemplating who most wants to replace you with an Egyptian ruler.
    Do you make a list of:
    - ❏ a. the pros and cons of each person close to you? (*rational*)
    - ❏ b. varied comments from friends and relatives on what they say behind your back regarding how your influence them and what they want from you? (*enthusiastic*)

20. You're the scribe trying to solve Toot's murder in ancient Egypt.
    Would you rather investigate:
    - ❏ a. the tried-and-true facts about Aye? (*grounded*)
    - ❏ b. what's in the overall picture before you fill in the clues? (*verve*)

21. You're a scribe painting Toot's tomb shortly after his demise.
    Would you:
    - ❏ a. seldom make errors of detail when looking for clues such as taking notice of Aye's wedding present to the young, healthy queen: her freshly inscribed coffin? (*grounded*)
    - ❏ b. prefer more innovative work, such as writing secret love poems to the queen disguised as prayers and watching for Toot's ghost to escape through the 8-inch-square hole cut in the rock of his tomb? (*verve*)

22. As a scribe in ancient Egypt, do you become tired when:
    - ❏ a. you work alone all day in a dimly torch-lit tomb? (*outgoing*)
    - ❏ b. King Toot interrupts your concentration on your work to demand that you greet and entertain his guests all evening at banquets? (*loner*)

23. When the queen asks you as a scribe to write love poems for her that she can hand to Toot, do you:
   - ❏ a. create the ideas for your poems by long discussions with the queen? (*outgoing*)
   - ❏ b. prefer to be alone when you reach deep down inside your spirit to listen to what your Ka and Ba (soul entities) tell you as the only resource for writing metaphors? (*loner*)

24. You are in ancient Egypt investigating the death of Toot. Do you prefer to:
   - ❏ a. question many different foreigners and locals at boisterous celebrations in different languages? (*outgoing*)
   - ❏ b. disregard outside events and look inside the family history/genealogy inscriptions on a stellae for the culprit? (*loner*)

25. King Toot at age 9 asks you to develop ideas for him about how to act when ascending the throne so young. Do you prefer to develop ideas through:
   - ❏ a. reflection, meditation, and prayer? (*loner*)
   - ❏ b. discussions and interviews among Toot's playmates on what makes Toot laugh? (*outgoing*)

26. As a scribe, are you:
   - ❏ a. rarely cautious about the family position of those with whom you socialize as long as they are kind, righteous people who do good deeds? (*outgoing*)
   - ❏ b. seeking one person with power to raise you from scribe to governor of Egypt, if only the pharaoh would ask your advice? (*loner*)

27. You are a sculptor in ancient Egypt when the pharaoh asks you to carve a name for yourself on a marble column that's a special representation of its owner. Would you:
   - ❏ a. inscribe the hieroglyph that means "remote"? (*loner*)
   - ❏ b. choose a special name for yourself that means "he who shares time easily with many foreigners"? (*outgoing*)

28. As an ancient scribe, do you work better when you:
   - ❏ a. spend your day off where no one can see you, asking the Sphinx why its claws are so sharp and made of reef-formed limestone? (*loner*)
   - ❏ b. spend your free time training teams of apprentice scribes to sculpt their own faces? (*outgoing*)

29. If you discovered a new land, would you build your cities upon:
   - ❏ a. your wise elders' principles, as they always have worked well before? (*traditional*)
   - ❏ b. unfamiliar cargo that traders brought from afar to your land? (*change-driven*)

30. Would you depict your king's victories on a stone column exactly as:
    - ❑ a. surviving witnesses from both sides recounted the events? (*change-driven*)
    - ❑ b. the pharaoh wants people to see? (*traditional*)

31. If you're self-motivated, would you avoid learning from your overseer because your overseer doesn't:
    - ❑ a. keep up with the times? (*change-driven*)
    - ❑ b. let you follow in your father's footsteps? (*traditional*)

32. Would you prefer to:
    - ❑ a. train scribes, because your father taught you how to do it well? (*traditional*)
    - ❑ b. move quickly from one project to another forever? (*change-driven*)

33. Do you feel like an outsider when:
    - ❑ a. you think more about the future than about current chores? (*change-driven*)
    - ❑ b. invaders replace your forefathers' familiar foods with unfamiliar cuisine? (*traditional*)

34. Do you quickly:
    - ❑ a. solve problems for those inside when you're coming from outside? (*change-driven*)
    - ❑ b. refuse to spend your treasures to develop new ideas that might fail? (*traditional*)

35. Would you rather listen to and learn from philosophers who:
    - ❑ a. predict a future in which old habits are replaced with new ones? (*change-driven*)
    - ❑ b. are only interested in experiencing one day at a time? (*traditional*)

Self-Scoring the Test

Add up the number of answers for each of the following 10 writing style traits for the 35 questions. There are seven questions for each group. The 10 categories are made up of these five opposite pairs: *grounded vs. verve, rational vs. enthusiastic, decisive vs. investigative, loner vs. outgoing,* and *traditional vs. change-driven.*

Put the numbers for each answer next to the categories. (See the self-scored test and results that follow.)

Total Grounded:	_____	Total Verve:	_____
Total Rational:	_____	Total Enthusiastic:	_____
Total Decisive:	_____	Total Investigative:	_____
Total Loner:	_____	Total Outgoing:	_____
Total Traditional:	_____	Total Change-Driven:	_____

Scoring Example

1.	b	verve	13.	a	enthusiastic	25.	b	outgoing
2.	a	enthusiastic	14.	a	investigative	26.	a	outgoing
3.	b	verve	15.	b	investigative	27.	b	outgoing
4.	a	enthusiastic	16.	a	investigative	28.	a	loner
5.	a	enthusiastic	17.	b	investigative	29.	b	change-driven
6.	b	verve	18.	b	enthusiastic	30.	b	traditional
7.	b	investigative	19.	b	enthusiastic	31.	a	change-driven
8.	b	investigative	20.	b	verve	32.	b	change-driven
9.	a	investigative	21.	b	verve	33.	a	change-driven
10.	b	verve	22.	b	loner	34.	a	change-driven
11.	b	enthusiastic	23.	b	loner	35.	b	traditional
12.	b	verve	24.	b	loner			

Scores

Total Grounded:	0	Total Verve:	5
Total Rational:	0	Total Enthusiastic:	7
Total Decisive:	0	Total Investigative:	7
Total Loner:	4	Total Outgoing:	3
Total Traditional:	2	Total Change-Driven:	5

The five highest numbers of answers are enthusiastic, investigative, change-driven, verve, and loner. Choose the highest numbers first as having the most importance (or weight) in your writing style preference. Therefore, your own *creative writing style and the way you plot your character's actions, interests, and goals* (for fiction writing and specifically mystery writing) is an ***enthusiastic investigative vivacious (verve-with-imagination/change-driven) loner.***

Your five personality letters would be: E I V L C. (Scramble the letters to make a word to remember—such as the name Clive, in this case.)

Note that there is a tie between **C** and V. Both have a score of 5. However, because V (verve), which signifies vivacious imagination with gusto, competes with **C**, being change-driven, the verve in the vivacious personality wracked with creative imagination would wither in a traditional corporation that emphasizes routinely running a tight ship. Traditional firms seek to imitate successful corporations of the past that worked well and still work. They don't need to be fixed often unless they make noise.

Instead, the dominantly change-driven creative individual would flourish better with a forward-looking, trend-setting creative corporation and build security from flexibility of job skill. When in doubt, turn to action verbs to communicate your *drive*. If you're misplaced, you won't connect as well with co-workers and may be dubbed a "loose canon."

You know you're in the right job when your personality connects with the group to share meaning. Communication is the best indicator of your personality matching a corporation's character traits. It's all about connecting more easily.

Your main character or alter-ego could probably be an enthusiastic, investigative, imaginative loner. But you'd not only have lots of imagination and creativity, but also verve, that vivacious gusto. You'd have fervor, dash, and élan.

The easily excitable, investigative, creative/imaginative loner described as having verve is more likely to represent what you feel inside your core personality, your self-insight, as you explore your own values and interests.

It's what you feel, what your *values* represent on this test at this moment in time. That's how a lot of personality tests work. This one is customized for fiction writers. Another test could be tailored for career area interests or for analyzing what stresses you. Think of your personality as your virtues.

Qualities of the test-taker represent more of a sentimental, charismatic, imaginative, investigative individual who likes to work alone most of the time. The person could at times be more change-driven than traditional. The real test is whether the test-taker is consistent about these traits or values on many different assessments of interests, personality, or values.

What's being tested here is imaginative fiction writing style. Writing has a personality, genre, or character of its own. The writing style and values are revealed in the way the characters drive the plot.

These sample test scores measure the preference, interest, and trait of the writer. The tone and mood are measured in this test. It's a way of sharing meaning, of communicating by driving the characters and the plot in a selected direction.

This assessment "score" reveals a fiction writer who is enthusiastically investigative in tone, mood, and texture. These traits or values apply to the writer as well as to the primary characters in the story.

The traits driving a writer's creativity also drive the main characters. Writer and characters work in a partnership of alter egos to move the plot forward. A creativity test lets you select and express the action, attitudes, and values of the story in a world that you shape according to clues, critical thinking, and personal likes.

？ ？ ？ ？ ？ ？ ？ ？

Appendix B

Anne Hart's Communicator's Job Task Interest Classifier

The classifier consists of 28 questions designed to measure your preferred style of writing and relationships at work for all types of communicators: writers, editors, journalists, indexers, publicists, communications-related educators, human resources personnel, interviewers, researchers, and speakers. Each question presents two possible answers. There are no right or wrong answers—only differences in personality preferences measured in shades of gray.

Use your score to match your personality preference with the preferences of potential employers or teammates, or use for team-building exercises. Fit your own interests, traits, or preferences with what's required of you on the job and as you interact with your peers at work.

Instructions

1. Read each possible answer, and place a check mark in the corresponding box to mark your preferred response. Leave the other box blank.

2. Count the number of a answers and b answers, and transfer those to the appropriate place in the scoring section.

3. After you have answered all the questions, transfer your totals to the score sheet.

Have fun. Enjoy the assessment.

1. You would rather promote your latest book by _____.
   - ❑ a. an author tour
   - ❑ b. online chats

2. Where will your research start for your next article or book?
   - ❑ a. interviewing out in the field
   - ❑ b. recording your inner hunch

3. Most of your ideas for writing reflect _____.
   - ❑ a. your internal feelings or thoughts
   - ❑ b. current issues in the news about people

4. What kind of relationship would you like with your publisher?
   - ❑ a. direct contact by phone
   - ❑ b. indirect contact via e-mail

5. How do you feel after conducting an interview?
   - ❑ a. energized enough to open more doors
   - ❑ b. exhausted enough to meditate in seclusion

6. Which article interests you enough to research?
   - ❑ a. a question-and-answer interview
   - ❑ b. a collection of one-line quotes.

7. Which work style would interest you most?
   - ❑ a. collaboration with teammates over lunch
   - ❑ b. working alone on a book at your own pace

8. In investigating and reporting crime news, which set of clues would you prefer to finally expose the culprit?
   - ❑ a. dates and facts on the culprit's letters
   - ❑ b. your own inner hunch about the culprit's personality

9. You would rather write _____.
   - ❑ a. practical, how-to articles or books
   - ❑ b. books or reports that forecast trends

10. Which company feels like the best-fit workplace?
    - ❑ a. a traditional periodical with a fact-checker
    - ❑ b. a socially bold venture capitalist pushing the limits

11. If you were an editor-in-chief, which job would you want?
    - ❑ a. edit a trendy fashion, sports, or travel magazine
    - ❑ b. edit industrial, government, or technical trade journals

12. When writing professionally, you would rather _____.
    - ❑ a. keep sentences under 10 words with bulleted lists
    - ❑ b. use metaphors and mind-mapping visuals

13. You most often write about _____.
   - ❑ a. the process
   - ❑ b. the result

14. Which would you rather review?
   - ❑ a. a textbook, guidebook, or manual
   - ❑ b. a novel

15. How do you decide?
   - ❑ a. by reasoning, thinking, or logic
   - ❑ b. by gut hunches

16. Which topic would most interest you?
   - ❑ a. entertainment law
   - ❑ b. story-telling

17. Which would you rather see your byline on?
   - ❑ a. *Amazing True Life Story Confessions Magazine*
   - ❑ b. *Rough Terrain Wheelchair Technology Design Magazine*

18. You would rather write or edit for a publisher who _____.
   - ❑ a. outsmarts the competition with 10 proven tactics
   - ❑ b. cultivates creative expression brainstorming lunches

19. You would rather write about _____.
   - ❑ a. new applications of artificial intelligence and heuristics
   - ❑ b. virtual reality therapy for agoraphobia

20. Which topic would you rather investigate as your new hobby?
   - ❑ a. niche or ethnic romance online
   - ❑ b. robots, avatars, and smart agents online

21. Your editor returns your completed manuscript with shocking changes. How do you feel?
   - ❑ a. You appreciate the feedback because it leads to improvement in the work and in your reputation.
   - ❑ b. Your feelings would be hurt by criticism of the real you.

22. Visitors to your Website or office will find _____.
   - ❑ a. well-organized files and outlines
   - ❑ b. spontaneous surprises

23. Which is a better description of your favorite editor?
    ❑ a. makes changes up to the last minute
    ❑ b. plans revisions well in advance

24. You manage your writing time by _____.
    ❑ a. prioritizing cycles of work and rest
    ❑ b. working in spurts when inspired by something you see

25. You'll promote your new book by _____.
    ❑ a. serializing the chapters for magazines
    ❑ b. selling it to the highest bidder in a silent auction

26. Which full-time job do you prefer for the next four decades?
    ❑ a. freelance writing, editing, or indexing (no pension, insurance, or benefits)
    ❑ b. staff employment as a writer (full-time, with pension, insurance, and benefits)

27. Which project is your favorite?
    ❑ a. an interactive workshop online
    ❑ b. a tutorial guaranteed to improve your writing

28. For which company would you rather work?
    ❑ a. an old-money corporation running a tight ship that's steeped in tradition and rarely changing the repetition of your editorial and public relations job duties
    ❑ b. a small, very creative business that changes direction on the fly with each new project you're assigned but could close if it loses funding or bread-and-butter clients

How to Self-Score the Communicator's Job Task Interest Classifier

To score the classifier, add up the number of "a" answers and "b" answers, and enter the sums in the "TOTAL" boxes below.

Total A answers [   ]   Total B answers [   ]

Transfer your totals to the appropriate section in the following chart.

Description	A Answers ☐	B Answers ☐
Part I: This score indicates whether you are more of a loner or more outgoing. Outgoing people usually enjoy being generalists who focus on breadth of knowledge, whereas loners usually feel happier and more comfortable at work being specialists, emphasizing depth of knowledge—but with versatility in fields related to or used in their specialty. A loner doesn't like to be constantly supervised or micromanaged. Loners, as introverts, feel stressed, drained, and wary or anxious by constant contact with people. Outgoing people are more at home with a wider variety of strangers and do not need to recharge before meeting strangers. Outgoing extroverts quickly find a connection and rapport with new clients, and they easily communicate with others.	Loner (L)	Outgoing (O)
Part II: This score determines whether you prefer to absorb real-world, present-day practical details through your vision, touch, smell, and hearing, or would rather take in theoretical, abstract information based on ideas or faith instead of present or historical proven facts. Grounded, down-to-earth people take in details by seeing, hearing, smelling or touching tangible objects. Individuals with verve are vivacious, imaginative people full of gusto who prefer to take in information by focusing on the intangible ideas and abstract theories, vision, and beliefs of what could be possible with a extra exploration of what is real about reality. Those with verve prefer to state that our eyes or memory could deceive us regarding reality. Grounded, down-to-earth people may not have as much verve, but they do have gumption and drive. They prefer to state concisely information	Grounded (G)	Verve (V)

Description	A Answers	B Answers
that they can verify, see, touch, hear, or smell as reality. Grounded individuals need to know that the facts aren't flawed.		
Part III: This score shows whether your judgment is based on rational or enthusiastic processes. Enthusiastic people make decisions based on their gut feelings. Rational people decide according to a list of pros and cons. They weigh the negatives against the positives on their list and go with the greatest number when they add up the negatives and compare them against the positives on a laundry list before making a decision. Rational people tell us to use our brain more and our reactions to events less before we act or make a decision. Rational fellows focus on critical thinking. Enthusiastic people emphasize speaking their minds, listening to healing sounds, going with the flow of gut hunches, favorite dramas, cargo magic, mind-body-spirit research, body movements, connecting, and the sixth sense.	Rational (R)	Enthusiastic (E)
Part IV: This score reveals your tolerance for ambiguity and change. Decisive people are well organized, are methodical, and need to make quick decisions under the pressure of reduced time and stress. They may overlook vital information that they didn't take time to evaluate. By deciding so quickly, they could hit a blind spot that could derail their executive careers early on. They have to learn to make decisions only after looking over the most valuable information needed to make a decision. Investigative people, on the other hand, like to wait until all the facts are in before making a decision. They enjoy investigating all the possibilities or alternatives before closing the book or signing the contracts. They don't want to overlook something important.	Decisive (D)	Investigative (I)

Description	A Answers ☐	B Answers ☐

Part V:
     This score reveals how much you prefer to be driven by tradition or driven by a need for constant change. An example of a change-driven person would be a need to keep working on a new project frequently.
 	
     No sooner is your last project finished then you want to forget about it and go on to the next project. You'd do best in a job or your own business where you can work on different projects that gave you a chance to learn new information or skills.
 	
     If you're a traditional person rather than a change-driven individual, you'd be better off looking for work with a traditional company that offers you the security you need. It's more important to stay with a company and grow as long as you have the health insurance, promotions, benefits, vacations, pensions, and perks.
 	
     You wouldn't mind routine job tasks as much as the change-driven person. If you want to work for a forward-looking, change-driven firm that offers less security but more chance to explore, look for surprises with companies that are forward-looking or those that focus on new trends, such as think tanks. You won't be happy doing the same routine all day such as teaching the same subject year after year or routine clerical tasks that never seem to change in scope.
	Traditional (T)	Change-Driven (C)

    Circle the letter of the category with the higher number in each of parts I through V.

    Then write those letters in the corresponding blank spaces to reveal your personality preference.

    Congratulations! You're an ____ ____ ____ ____ ____

? ? ? ? ? ? ? ?

Appendix C

Sample Anger Test

Instructions:

Check the boxes as to whether you strongly agree, sometimes agree, or strongly disagree

1. I never have lost a buddy.
   ❏ strongly agree   ❏ sometimes agree   ❏ strongly disagree

2. I always have liked my boss.
   ❏ strongly agree   ❏ sometimes agree   ❏ strongly disagree

3. I have never acted on an impulse to eat sweets.
   ❏ strongly agree   ❏ sometimes agree   ❏ strongly disagree

4. I have never lost my temper.
   ❏ strongly agree   ❏ sometimes agree   ❏ strongly disagree

5. I have never felt tired after work.
   ❏ strongly agree   ❏ sometimes agree   ❏ strongly disagree

6. I never have disliked a teacher.
   ❏ strongly agree   ❏ sometimes agree   ❏ strongly disagree

7. I never have voiced a comment after a speeding car pulled out in front of me.
   ❏ strongly agree   ❏ sometimes agree   ❏ strongly disagree

8. I never have spoken back to a parent.
   ❏ strongly agree   ❏ sometimes agree   ❏ strongly disagree

9. I never have been bored at work.
   ❏ strongly agree   ❏ sometimes agree   ❏ strongly disagree

10. I never have been annoyed by another person.
    ❏ strongly agree   ❏ sometimes agree   ❏ strongly disagree

11. I never have arrived anywhere late.
   ❏ strongly agree   ❏ sometimes agree   ❏ strongly disagree

12. I always have enjoyed school.
   ❏ strongly agree   ❏ sometimes agree   ❏ strongly disagree

13. I always have admired celebrities.
   ❏ strongly agree   ❏ sometimes agree   ❏ strongly disagree

14. I always have finished what I started.
   ❏ strongly agree   ❏ sometimes agree   ❏ strongly disagree

15. I always have been complimented on my work.
   ❏ strongly agree   ❏ sometimes agree   ❏ strongly disagree

16. I always have had the highest grades in school.
   ❏ strongly agree   ❏ sometimes agree   ❏ strongly disagree

17. I always have been hired for any job to which I applied.
   ❏ strongly agree   ❏ sometimes agree   ❏ strongly disagree

18. I have never lied.
   ❏ strongly agree   ❏ sometimes agree   ❏ strongly disagree

19. I always excelled in all my school subjects.
   ❏ strongly agree   ❏ sometimes agree   ❏ strongly disagree

20. I never have uttered a shock word for emphasis.
   ❏ strongly agree   ❏ sometimes agree   ❏ strongly disagree

21. I never have wanted to pet an animal.
   ❏ strongly agree   ❏ sometimes agree   ❏ strongly disagree

22. I always have tried to control all events around me.
   ❏ strongly agree   ❏ sometimes agree   ❏ strongly disagree

23. I always have been the best person for the job.
   ❏ strongly agree   ❏ sometimes agree   ❏ strongly disagree

24. I always have liked taking tests.
   ❏ strongly agree   ❏ sometimes agree   ❏ strongly disagree

25. I always have enjoyed taking orders or being reminded to do chores.
   ❏ strongly agree   ❏ sometimes agree   ❏ strongly disagree

Remember the "strongly agree" or "strongly disagree" answers sometimes raise red flags on tests of anger and sometimes on tests of honesty. Be on the lookout for "always" and "never" statements. (Refer back to Chapter 8 for a more in-depth discussion.)

? ? ? ? ? ? ? ?

Appendix D

Interests-in-Common
Classifier

Instructions:

Choose the answer that best suits what you'd rather do—in other words, what you prefer.

1. You get a phone call from a blind date. You plan to go out for fun on a Saturday night.
    You would rather:
    - ❑ a. actively go ethnic folk dancing, line dancing, or square dancing in a wholesome, crowded coffee house.
    - ❑ b. play video games alone while your date watches, or have you and your date order take-out food and sit in your living room playing games only two people can play. You take the phone off the hook and don't answer any doorbells from solicitors. You dislike when people disturb you and your date.

    (*outgoing or reflective*)

2. Computers are your hobby. At work you have time to show your hobby to your future mate during your two-hour lunch break in your flexible-time job. You choose to:
    - ❑ a. play virtual-reality martial arts video games as a sport purely for entertainment.
    - ❑ b. design programs for forecasting the weather daily for 100 years into the future.

    (*codified or abstruse*)

3. You would enjoy a soul mate who:
    ❑ a. selects from many details in planning your wedding and points out which details need improvement in shape, texture, mood, or color, and keep accurate records of facts.
    ❑ b. enjoys planning an ancient-themed wedding that entails making farfetched decisions about Egyptian coronation wedding theories. You might enjoy discussing ideas and attitudes that people have about marriage in different times and geographic locations.

    (*codified or abstruse*)

4. You have a date with two possible future mates. Because you want to choose very own soul mate and possible marriage partner according to whether that person's interests more exactly matches yours, you would choose:
    ❑ a. the mate (male or female) whose job is to analyze stocks and stock market trends, and apply artificial intelligence strategies to forecast upturn or downturn and who also analyzes computer systems using impersonal, objective logic all day.
    ❑ b. the mate more interested in what makes people tick who works as a director of human resource development. That mate uses a gifted understanding of people to head the personnel department or research training and human relations in the corporation. That mate's main duty is to place the right people in the best jobs.

    (*logical or sentimental*)

5. You work with someone you'd like to date, someone who you'd hope to marry, if things worked out right. At work, you're told to fire this person for taking too long to come back after maternity/paternity leave. You:
    ❑ a. terminate the person as ordered, telling the employee that the company cannot afford the loss of productivity and profit directly attributed to the individual's absence, but it's only fair that you two can go on dating and deepening your relationship as that person would make you a good future spouse.
    ❑ b. refuse to terminate the person as ordered. Out of empathy you advise the employee to sue the company for family leave discrimination and side with the person because of circumstances. You ask that person out on a date and tell him or her of your romantic intentions and hopes that a meaningful and deep relationship leading to marriage could be a possibility.

    (*logical or sentimental*)

6. When asked to shop on your lunch hour for your boss, you:
   - ❏ a. visit many different stores all day looking for exactly the right product at the best price and quality.
   - ❏ b. impulsively buy the first overpriced item you see that fills your boss's requirements so you can take the rest of the afternoon off to play and have fun. You tell your boss you had to spend the time hunting down exactly the right thing at the right price to save money.

   (*meticulous or waiting*)

7. You paid a nonrefundable $200 last month to reserve a ticket to attend a career-related convention five months from the present in Las Vegas. Today you found out there's a singles-only (your preferred age group) mystery writer's convention on the same day in Rio de Janeiro that you'd rather attend because it's more exciting.
   You are:
   - ❏ a. comfortable sticking to your original plans to attend the Las Vegas career networking convention because it doesn't require change.
   - ❏ b. feel deprived of an open-ended exciting experience, and wish you could afford to lose the $200 and take off for Rio de Janeiro at a moment's notice instead.

   (*meticulous or waiting*)

8. To give yourself more visibility among singles you'd like to meet you'd take:
   - ❏ a. a paid weekend job hosting a two-hour radio talk show, answering questions on the air about computers or software in your specialty.
   - ❏ b. a two-hour weekend job writing a singles column for newspaper about your own interests, reading, reflections, or research.

   (*outgoing or reflective*)

9. You would take an assignment in order to have:
   - ❏ a. job security and a high salary to spend any way you please.
   - ❏ b. the chance to have your work made into a film and plenty of worldwide recognition at conventions, but only a $1,500 pittance for your work.

   (*codified or abstruse*)

10. You'd rather take a mate whose interests match your:
    - ❏ a. realistic attitude and practical skills in keeping records.
    - ❏ b. imagination to create movies that sell escape.

    (*codified or abstruse*)

11. You wish you would have majored in a subject at college that:

❑ a. allowed you to decide logically and objectively in order to analyze strategies, map out models, or keep records to solve problems about production and profit at work.

❑ b. gave you the warm fuzzies from understanding what people value most about their careers.

(logical or sentimental)

12. If you knew you would be offered a great job after graduation, you would focus on the following five specialties within a college major:

❑ a. systems analysis, programming, logic, science, and math.

❑ b. illustration, professional writing, creativity studies, psychology, and human resource management.

(logical or sentimental)

13. Your supervisor gives you an assignment to write an article for the company's in-house employee newsletter on 10 home-based businesses you can operate with your personal computer.
You would prefer to:

❑ a. create a plan and outline first, follow it exactly to organize the article, and then write the article.

❑ b. write the article first, from whatever springs into your head at the moment. Then weed out what doesn't belong when it's finished.

(meticulous or waiting)

14. You're researching an international electronic database for a long list of articles and books on abductions of young people in Russia for an Ivy League university professor of psychiatry. You get a call from a Nobel prize–winning astrophysicist in your city asking you to stop your work immediately before he leaves the country and tape record what he has to say about asteroids and comets heading towards the Earth but not visible for the next 50 years.
You prefer to:

❑ a. finish your research for your psychiatrist-employer and tell the astrophysicist you'll write to him later. It's annoying to have to stop in the middle of a project and switch to a new task.

❑ b. drop what you're doing and look forward to the surprise, change in routine, and excitement of taping the astrophysicist's startling statistics on a different subject. You love going on to a new project quickly after you've finished the last one. You're already tired and bored from researching one topic and long to move on to a new subject to investigate and learn.

(meticulous or waiting)

15. You meet many possible mates at a series of parties who ask whether you're married, what you majored in, what your hobbies are, what you do for fun, and how old you are because they want to know you better. All of them could be Mr. or Ms. Right Personality Type, a possible future spouse for you. You tell the strangers:

❑ a. everything you can think of about yourself. You reveal all that interests you. You ask all the strangers to lunch and want to know all the details of their lives.

❑ b. you're a private person and don't want to reveal personal information, but you'll gladly ask the strangers questions about anything related to their interests.

(*outgoing or reflective*)

16. You want a high-paying, prestigious job or business of your own that uses all you have to offer and that you'll be able to keep until:

❑ a. you retire in 40 years with major benefits such as health insurance, a paid-off home mortgage, and a livable pension.

❑ b. a better job offers you an opportunity to use your wild imagination yearning for adventure, change, intellectual achievement and/or creative expression, and the next future possibility.

(*codified or abstruse*)

17. On Thursdays, your workplace lets all employees out at four to attend personal enrichment classes. You have a choice of two workshops. You would attend:

❑ a. How to Repair Your Home Appliances or Computer.

❑ b. How to Write Novels About the Future of Employment.

(*codified or abstruse*)

18. You are asked to evaluate an employee. You would first consider the employee's:

❑ a. productivity and profit to the firm.

❑ b. warmth, friendship, and personal service toward the customer.

(*logical or sentimental*)

19. You have a choice of working for two supervisors. You would prefer:

❑ a. the boss who talks to you *straight* about dating his adult child, but uses harsh words and sarcasm to make you improve your image but not your income while keeping you from getting personal or asking questions about his adult child or a raise.

❑ b. the *meek* boss who tells polite lies to protect you from knowing why your work was rejected. Then your boss asks the top honcho to reprimand you for errors. Finally, the boss approves of your dating interest in his grown child, but tells the honcho behind your back that you're a social climber trying to worm your way into the family.

(*logical or sentimental*)

20. Your job finishes at 5:00 p.m., but your departing manager says you can leave early if you want or hang around and start tomorrow's work. You won't be paid extra or less either way. No one's left in the office to see you working. You:

❑   a. start tomorrow's work and leave exactly at five, according to your usual daily schedule. You'll know exactly which place to start again in the morning with no confusion.

❑   b. drop everything in midstream, take off, and head for that new movie you're eager to see. Leave tomorrow's work for tomorrow, and have fun when you can grab it.

(meticulous or waiting)

21. You work in a field you simply love with many singles in your age group around, making life exciting. Your work is always:

❑   a. completed and well organized long before the deadline.

❑   b. finished exactly at deadline or just after. You enjoy the exhilaration of rushing to complete it on time.

(meticulous or waiting)

22. You're more comfortable:

❑   a. giving an oral presentation and live hands-on demonstration on opening doors for people to a large group of eligible singles of all ages in your company conference auditorium. You want to make that special other notice you. You love talking face to face with large groups of people who share your interests and hope a romance works out of this meeting.

❑   b. distributing the latest written book or newsletter you wrote to that special person and/or other students. You wish they could learn independently in school, at their own place of employment, or at home. You find giving an oral presentation to a group positively exhausting. You'd rather train students online or by assigning students to read what you write (books, manuals, articles, or newsletters) as part of a correspondence course. Public speaking makes you sick.

(outgoing or reflective)

23. In marriage, or within a family unit, you'd be happier as:

❑   a. one dependable business-focused logistics mate grounded in the present time and the real world who deals with troubleshooting and repair household appliances and remodeling; or in the sorting and selection of details in doing your spouse's taxes and financial planning.

❑   b. a future-looking absent-minded professor who uses neural networks technology from the biotech industry to create new possibilities classifying people as the most compatible mates to create the healthiest, happiest children.

(codified or abstruse)

24. You bought an old car or antique lamp at the best price you could find. Three years later you still:
    - ❑ a. use your car or lamp as is. If it isn't broken, you don't need to fix it or change it.
    - ❑ b. continue to upgrade your car or lamp to keep up with technology, tastes, or styles. Everything has room for improvement and change.

    (*codified or abstruse*)

25. When asked what you think of the concept of time, you're most likely to say that time
    - ❑ a. is impersonal.
    - ❑ b. makes you feel guilty if you don't use it to help people.

    (*logical or sentimental*)

26. There are two job openings: one for a spy and the other for a journalist. You have all the qualifications for both.
    You choose to:
    - ❑ a. design software to track government legal cases on harassment in politics and to merge databases with a secretly modified "back door" to allow intelligence agencies to access foreign computer systems for their own espionage purposes.
    - ❑ b. be a journalist who achieves visibility while investigating healthcare injustices, welfare scandals, and law-enforcement brutality.

    (*logical or sentimental*)

27. You find it easier to:
    - ❑ a. follow directions exactly as planned or told to you by others at work. You prefer looking at the other person's plans or schedules and following them as directed. You'd rather do the company's thing.
    - ❑ b. break regulations and do the work your own way. You find it harder to follow someone else's plans to the letter because you can't get into the other guy's head to know what he wants, and there's no way you can please him. When you try to follow others' rules, the work comes out wrong. You'd rather do your own thing.

    (*meticulous or waiting*)

28. You're better at:
    - ❑ a. time management of your home life after work.
    - ❑ b. adapting your workplace job to unexpected changes in your mate's or family's home-life schedule.

    (*meticulous or waiting*)

29. The job that would be least stressful is the:
    - ❑ a. receptionist guiding heavy foot traffic all day in and out of a novel publisher's public relations or sales office, answering constantly ringing phones while typing reports and press releases and running errands.
    - ❑ b. back-office word-processing specialist in a quiet but successful and long-standing one-person serious mainstream fiction publishing office where the boss usually is out and no one comes in or calls. You can have total solitude as you type one long mainstream novel after the other.

    (*outgoing or reflective*)

30. You'd be a mate whose conversations with your spouse would more naturally be about topics or people focusing on:
    - ❑ a. common sense, present, practical, useful, direct, realistic, actual, down-to earth, factual, specific, and traditional events.
    - ❑ b. futuristic, conceptual, inspirational, motivational, random, possible, intellectual, kooky, imaginative, fantastic, theoretical, ingenious, generalized, non-traditional, and creative events.

    (*codified or abstruse*)

31. The toy manufacturing company where you're employed is adding a corporate animation department. You're offered a choice of two jobs. You decide to take the job as a:
    - ❑ a. marketing and sales manager of toys.
    - ❑ b. designer and researcher of animated, holiday-themed robot cartoon characters, and scriptwriter of commercials.

    (*codified or abstruse*)

32. Your lover says you would prefer to do what's:
    - ❑ a. fair and truthful than do what will make your lover happy.
    - ❑ b. needed and valued to make your lover "like" you or to accommodate your lover's family and friends.

    (*logical or sentimental*)

33. It's more important to you to:
    - ❑ a. know you are right and not care whether you are liked.
    - ❑ b. be liked, and know you are right, even if everyone thinks you're wrong.

    (*logical or sentimental*)

34. You want a marriage where you can:
    - ❏ a. thrive on order and know pretty well what your home life relationships will be like.
    - ❏ b. explore the unknown without being pinned down. You want to keep all home life and relationship options open.

    (*meticulous or waiting*)

35. You prefer to spend blizzard weather weekends at home:
    - ❏ a. completing projects and getting them out of the way by the end of each day.
    - ❏ b. turning your home-based projects into play. You believe if your work can't be play, you won't do that particular job.

    (*meticulous or waiting*)

36. You ask to be placed in the:
    - ❏ a. sales department, to use your telephone skills.
    - ❏ b. publications department, working alone editing new information in your area of interest.

    (*outgoing or reflective*)

37. If you were promised the same salary and job security, you'd prefer to spend the next four decades:
    - ❏ a. dealing with details and your common sense instead of your imagination to fix what's broken on the job or be of service to people who need your help. You'd enjoy customer service, or checking, locating, or troubleshooting details for accuracy.
    - ❏ b. as an investigative journalist and suspense novelist who writes about the connections and interrelatedness between competing entertainment corporations. You use imagination to absorb global impressions or create new ideas.

    (*codified or abstruse*)

38. You pick your mate or date by making:
    - ❏ a. judgments based on past experience.
    - ❏ b. decisions based on gut-level guessing.

    (*codified or abstruse*)

39. The type of people you wish you could be more like are able to:
    - ❏ a. stay calm and objective when others panic.
    - ❏ b. walk 10 miles in your shoes.

    (*logical or sentimental*)

40. If you could pick a mate most like yourself, that person would:
    - ❑ a. welcome challenge, rebuttal, and confrontation, sacrificing harmony for clarity.
    - ❑ b. prefer harmony, even at the sake of sacrificing clarity to avoid conflict.

    (*logical or sentimental*)

41. You would prefer a mate who:
    - ❑ a. wants everything orderly and in its place—always.
    - ❑ b. doesn't plan to have a place for everything, because the adaptive person with messy closets and desks you are planning to marry would rather wait and see what living with you demands at different times.

    (*meticulous or waiting*)

42. You must interview blind dates in order to pick one to escort you on the world cruise for two you just won. Each applicant gets a half-hour interview. You now have only 10 minutes to choose the winner. You'd prefer each applicant to:
    - ❑ a. come only at the scheduled time of the interview.
    - ❑ b. walk in off the street when he felt like it and surprise you with his impressive credentials.

    (*meticulous or waiting*)

43. In a home-based business you'd prefer to:
    - ❑ a. run your own public relations, advertising, sales, and marketing agency for authors, doctors, or lawyers.
    - ❑ b. index the back of books and periodicals for doctors, lawyers, publishers, and library databases behind closed doors, where you'd work alone, with no close supervision and no phone calls or interruptions.

    (*outgoing or reflective*)

44. You find the future:
    - ❑ a. best put off until it comes because it's too scary.
    - ❑ b. full of exciting possibilities for your imagination.

    (*codified or abstruse*)

45. In your school classes you enjoyed best the courses that emphasized:
    - ❑ a. hands-on practical skills leading to a comfortable job in the real world as quickly as possible.
    - ❑ b. theory about the futuristic possibilities your mate might be capable of once microchips were enmeshed with human DNA molecules to form neural networks.

    (*codified or abstruse*)

46. All appliances/machines/electric power/phones break down at the same time. Your first impulse would be to:
    - ❑ a. keep things in perspective and push for precision and clarity when directing others to fix what's broken.
    - ❑ b. try to understand how human error impacts the people affected by the power meltdown.

    (logical or sentimental)

47. In a marriage, you'd rather:
    - ❑ a. solve analytical problems and increase efficiency.
    - ❑ b. express your creativity by sharing communication or service with a smile.

    (logical or sentimental)

48. You must choose your mate from among three suitable friends you've been dating for more than two years. Each gave you a deadline day, and an ultimatum to make your decision.
    You'd rather:
    - ❑ a. keep your decision goal-oriented and reach a closure as soon as possible for relief.
    - ❑ b. stay open-ended without goals because new information may come in before deadline.

    (meticulous or waiting)

49. As a newly hired writer with a B.A. in English, you're asked to manage the technical writing department. You never worked before and know nothing about technical writing. It's your first day at work.
    You would like to:
    - ❑ a. hurry permanent decisions, turn solutions into action, and implement communications right into the word-processing department.
    - ❑ b. keep the staff from going with the first decision, keep offering better solutions, and hold communications until you've cleared it with the technical illustration department—before turning the current iteration over to the word-processing department.

    (meticulous or waiting)

50. You just graduated from college. Two employers are eager to hire you. Each offer equal benefits. You'd rather:
    - ❑ a. use your natural, terrific public speaking skills to train *many people*, employees and students, in how to act a certain way at work to win friends and influence people, or how to do a certain job. You'd love to do lots of demonstrations and give great presentations for people. You think or communicate best on your feet.

❑ b. organize records for a healthcare management firm monitoring production runs and performing backups of corporate data working *alone*. Or illustrate, write, or edit magazine articles and children's books or current events and new trends reports, working *alone* for the communications and publications department.

(*outgoing or reflective*)

51. You prefer to work side by side with your mate at home in a hobby you love that deals mainly with using:

❑ a. practical, real, tangible, specific, common sense, hands-on troubleshooting skills based on practice, usefulness, and experience.

❑ b. your imagination and forecasting trends to show others how to find hidden escape routes, back doors, advantages, alternatives, theories, and new ways of doing things.

(*codified or abstruse*)

52. If you were a salesperson, you'd rather sell:

❑ a. tangible products, such as fashions, appliances, computers, modems, and peripherals; financial database software to accounting firms; or medical records technology and transcription software to hospitals.

❑ b. ideas, such as infomercials, advertising, public relations, public speaking, logos, desktop video productions, scripts, novels, graphic design concepts, event planning enterprises, artificial intelligence solutions, trend forecasting, interactive fiction, presentation graphics productions, and virtual reality games.

(*codified or abstruse*)

53. You're retired and contemplating marriage again to find happiness for the final third of your lifespan. Your dates are most likely to call you:

❑ a. a tough-skinned, hard-headed date who clawed your way to the top by your achievements, power, intelligence, persistence, and education.

❑ b. an empathic, persuasive self-made date who always put first—above your own desires—your friend's need. You live by your personal values and your own gut-reactions about people and situations.

(*logical or sentimental*)

54. You're asked to give a presentation to people with the same hobby as yours at a fun-filled, leisurely convention not connected to your job. You'd prefer to:

❑ a. convince the audience by logical analysis to clarify definitions, facts, or trends.

❑ b. persuade the people by communicating to their values, sentiment, and identity with a stirring videotape or film.

(*logical or sentimental*)

55. When searching for a mate, you:
    - ❏ a. grab the first date you find so fast that you're disappointed later.
    - ❏ b. switch relationships or dates as frequently as you switched majors in college or tech school.

    (*meticulous or waiting*)

56. You want a good marriage partner who is:
    - ❏ a. reliable, stable, serious, secure, unchanging, controllable, orderly, routine, familiar, scheduled, methodical, organized, and dependable.
    - ❏ b. flexible, adaptable, leisurely, playful, fun, spontaneous, changeable, open-ended, and creative.

    (*meticulous or waiting*)

57. At your deepest level, lots of people contact activity after work or on vacation makes you feel:
    - ❏ a. energized and eager to talk and share your life experiences. Your phone and door are kept open for the sounds of people networking.
    - ❏ b. sick, drained, exhausted, anxious, tense, pressured, and bored by a continuous, crushing crowd on whom you wish you could close your door when you want some recreation and peace of mind after work or on weekends and vacations. You disconnect your phone.

    (*outgoing or reflective*)

58. If you learned how to design your own parlor game, you would:
    - ❏ a. produce a new product that will appreciate in value over the years, even when the board game becomes outdated. You'd patent the new product and save the profits in your retirement plan.
    - ❏ b. have some fun teaching kids how to use it and then donating the game to an imagination-stretching camp high in the mountains. Afterwards, you enjoy a vacation as a guest of the camp.

    (*codified or abstruse*)

59. You have a choice of two conferences to attend during the holiday season. You're lonely and single. Neither conference is related to your present job. You'd rather attend a conference on:
    - ❏ a. improving your practical skills that will allow you to pass a qualifying exam for a more secure job at a higher salary.
    - ❏ b. military abductions, advertising evidence presented by a distinguished military general, a Nobel prize–winning physicist, an Ivy League–university professor of psychiatry, and three security guards who witnessed autopsies on space aliens at a secret military testing site's underground base.

    (*codified or abstruse*)

60. When you criticize your date, mate, or yourself, you're more apt to see:
   ❑ a. the errors of clarity and organization, and how the person or his or her attitudes can be improved or made more efficient. You want to critique and analyze it, or see how and where the person's actions went wrong. You welcome challenge and rebuttal. You want a mate who makes objective and impersonal decisions.
   ❑ b. the way he or she motivates, inspires, excites, and persuades you to understand his or her feelings, personal values, likes and dislikes, choices, and attitudes by his or her smooth-talking style. You praise your mate or date for using propaganda in the home for meeting your needs for simplicity and harmony.

   (*logical or sentimental*)

61. You're hired to train the co-workers on your team and to mentor beginning students in your field of interest. You let the students know that you're more interested in the:
   ❑ a. subject than in the student's personal problems, learning needs, or motivation.
   ❑ b. students' personal needs and motivation, inspiration, and growth than you are in the subject.

   (*logical or sentimental*)

62. You'd rather enter a marriage where:
   ❑ a. every minute of your day is planned, and you use a day planner or make a list of what you'll do each day, including weekends and vacations. You wouldn't mind if your mate assigned you specific chores to do around the house, and you'd give your children chores to do around the house. You believe idle hands get into trouble, and the day is wasted if you don't get some work done. You don't mind following someone else's rules to the letter.
   ❑ b. you have many hours of free time to see what leisurely and spontaneous activities can be fun-filled or full of your creative expressions. Heaven help the mate who crushes your autonomy at home or asks you to work at something that doesn't interest you. Work at home or outside should be playful.

   (*meticulous or waiting*)

63. On weekends you:
   ❑ a. make a list of every chore that needs to be finished and every item you have to buy. You'll visit stores only when you need to buy a specific product on your list.

❑ b. let whatever happens spontaneously take over the day depending upon your energy level, who calls, or what movie is playing. You dread working on your free time, and prefer to see what fun happens as the weekend progresses. You'd rather browse.

(meticulous or waiting)

64 On your resume you would be certain to emphasize your:

❑ a. interest in giving presentations, speeches, or talks on your area of interest or experience.

❑ b. preference for communicating via the written word in memos to co-workers and as little face-to-face talking as possible.

(outgoing or reflective)

65. You'd rather take those thick, dry, dull books catching dust on university library shelves and

❑ a. review them for a practical, how-to, hands-on magazine.

❑ b. turn them into spectacular 60-minute multimedia instructional videos for beginners.

(codified or abstruse)

66. You'd rather repair:

❑ a. machines in buildings.

❑ b. attitudes of people.

(codified or abstruse)

67. You want to duck out the door and take a break when:

❑ a. your date or mate cries openly.

❑ b. you say something negative that you really mean and don't want to apologize.

(logical or sentimental)

68. You're a healthy, energetic age and forced to retire against your wishes to continue having fun in your occupation.
You wish you and your same-age mate could:

❑ a. analyze, challenge, and confront ageism with the truth.

❑ b. deny that ageism exists in your specialty and convey optimism, energy, and enthusiasm by affirming your desire to offer service for pay.

(logical or sentimental)

69. To propose marriage, you need most:
  - ❑ a. an agenda with handouts and flow charts.
  - ❑ b. room to move in all directions by self-pacing, a chance to change the agenda, and diverge from the original plan.

  (*meticulous or waiting*)

70. You'd rather listen to:
  - ❑ a. lectures about ideas on several theories of how life arose on Earth. You like listening to lectures about faith, imagination, fantasy, and compassion, and you enjoy radio or TV shows that discuss what are the most mature and sensible attitudes you can show for your mate and family.
  - ❑ b. **lectures** about self-determination, reason, rebellion, reality, and skepticism in the face of disagreement by the majority in your community or family. As a skeptic, you'd rather be right in your own mind than win in the eyes of others. You believe others want to be deceived if the deception offers comfort and reward.

  (*meticulous or waiting*)

71. You're always willing to:
  - ❑ a. share personal experiences by talking and expressing your opinions; volunteering to work on committees and attend meetings, functions, office parties, or after-work cultural or sports events; and speak on panels at conferences.
  - ❑ b. write an inner personal journal in which you research, reflect, meditate, and blow the whistle—especially when a co-worker or mate interrupts you in mid-paragraph. You'd not hesitate to write a published book about your mate.

  (*outgoing or reflective*)

72. On a first date you'd reveal:
  - ❑ a. only those realistic, practical, useful, routine, hands-on details about your skills. You'd hand a date your resume or talk about what you do at work.
  - ❑ b. your ideas, abilities, and examples of creativity or your favorite theories. You'd try to convince the date or partner to consider alternatives that don't yet exist in the present, to accommodate your values, inner worlds, or beliefs. You want to rush things, perhaps propose on the first date, but you keep silent because you don't want the other person to mistakenly think you're controlling.

  (*codified or abstruse*)

73. Your employer is giving you an "employee of the month" award. You'd prefer the prize to be:

    ❑ a. a win/lose award for beating out the rival firms.

    ❑ b. a psychology book on "why women see competition as loss of self."

    (*logical or sentimental*)

74. You spend too much time:

    ❑ a. making lists and pre-nuptial contracts in order to arrive at a quicker decision about who will become your partner or mate. You are concerned about whether you chose the right person for an important relationship because changes are upsetting.

    ❑ b. gathering endless information about other people, but not making any commitments or final decisions about a relationship, hoping new information (or a better prospect) comes your way. You believe time changes pre-nuptial contracts anyway, and verbal agreements are sufficient.

    (*meticulous or waiting*)

Interests-in-Common Classifier Key

O= Outgoing

R= Reflective

C= Codified

A= Abstruse

L= Logical

S= Sentimental

M= Meticulous

W= Waiting

Scoring the Interests-in-Common Classifier

To score your answer sheet, follow the sample scored sheet that contains the four preference letters **RASW**

As you can see, the questions have been separated by the preferences in the key. The higher number within each scoring section (outgoing vs. reflective, codified vs. abstruse, logical vs. sentimental, and meticulous vs. waiting) is the letter that stands for your preference.

Outgoing or Reflective

Question number	a (outgoing)	b (reflective)	Question number	a (outgoing)	b (reflective)
1	X		43		X
8	X		50		X
15	X		57		X
22		X	64	X	
29		X	71		X
36		X			
Subtotals	3	3		1	4
				3	3
			Total	4 O	7 R

Codified or Abstruse

Question number	a (codified)	b (abstruse)	Question number	a (codified)	b (abstruse)
2		X	38		X
3	X		44		X
9		X	45		X
10	X		51		X
16		X	52		X
17	X		58		X
23	X		59		X
24	X		65		X
30	X		66		X
31		X	72		X
37	X				
Subtotals	7	4		0	10
				7	4
			Total	7 C	14 A

Logical or Sentimental

Question number	a (logical)	b (sentimental)	Question number	a (logical)	b (sentimental)
4		X	40		**X**
5		X	46	X	
11		X	47		X
12	X		53	X	
18		X	54		X
19		X	60	X	
25		X	61	X	
26	X		67	X	
32		X	68	X	
33		X	73		X
39		X			
Subtotals	2	9		6	4
				2	9
			Total	8 L	13 S

Meticulous or Waiting

Question number	a (meticulous)	b (waiting)	Question number	a (meticulous)	b (waiting)
6	X		42		**X**
7		X	48		X
13	X		49		X
14		X	55		X
20	X		56		X
21		X	62		X
27	X		63		X
28		X	69		X
34		X	70		X
35		X	74		X
41		X			
Subtotals	4	7		0	10
				4	7
			Total	4 M	17 W

155

Your preferences are R A S W.

R shows that you're reflective, a person interested in self-insight and self-identity who is also introverted.

A is for abstruse, which means you're similar to other people who enjoy abstract theories and out-on-a-limb ideas emphasizing intuitive ideas.

S is for sentimental. The art of sentimental journeys relates to behavior such as care-giving, nourishing, and showing empathy. You're a reflective, sentimental "empath" who enjoys investigating hidden theoretical information such as the alternative health, nutrition, and the mind-body-spirit industry. Narrowed to only one industry, your focused interests would emphasize exploring music to see whether there are studies of how healing sounds relieve stress and foster healthier people and/or calmer environments.

The fourth letter, W, is for waiting. The waiting kind of person is symbolically represented by a front-loading ancillary—a trade journal. You wait for information so new the media hasn't touched it yet. Waiting is about seeking new trends, new theories, and new data before you arrive at any decisions. Information you wait for would be in your area of interest, your reading hobby, which emphasizes research in DNA-driven genealogy and personal history studies. You like to investigate and report. So W means waiting to investigate reliable research, and cross-checking the research again to be sure it isn't flawed. That's the making of an investigative reporter looking to explore new information and to spontaneously offer breaking news, hidden markets, or similar information.

Put all the letters together, and RASW spells a reflective, abstruse, sentimental person waiting with an open-minded attitude for facts to be checked, theories to be proven, and surprising news before making my choices.

Blank Interests-in-Common Classifier Score Sheet

Outgoing or Reflective

Question number	a (outgoing)	b (reflective)	Question number	a (outgoing)	b (reflective)
1			43		
8			50		
15			57		
22			64		
29			71		
36					
Subtotals					
		Total		O	R

Codified or Abstruse

Question number	a (codified)	b (abstruse)	Question number	a (codified)	b (abstruse)
2			38		
3			44		
9			45		
10			51		
16			52		
17			58		
23			59		
24			65		
30			66		
31			72		
37					
Subtotals					
Total				C	A

Logical or Sentimental

Question number	a (logical)	b (sentimental)	Question number	a (logical)	b (sentimental)
4			40		
5			46		
11			47		
12			53		
18			54		
19			60		
25			61		
26			67		
32			68		
33			73		
39					
Subtotals					
Total				L	S

Meticulous or Waiting

Question number	a (meticulous)	b (waiting)	Question number	a (meticulous)	b (waiting)
6			42		
7			48		
13			49		
14			55		
20			56		
21			62		
27			63		
28			69		
34			70		
35			74		
41					
Subtotals					
Total				M	W

Interests-in-Common Classifier Key

O= Outgoing

R= Reflective

C= Codified

A= Abstruse

L= Logical

S= Sentimental

M= Meticulous

W= Waiting

Your preferences are ___ ___ ___ ___.

? ? ? ? ? ? ? ?

Appendix E

Anne Hart's High-Tech/Low-Tech Career and Personality Preference Classifier

Read each of the work-related situations. Put an X or check mark next to either "a" or "b." To score your answers, total your "a" answers and your "b" answers, and transfer your totals to the personality category boxes that follow the test. (These pairs are marked O (outgoing) or L (loner); G (grounded) or V (verve); R (rational) or E (enthusiastic); D (decisive) or I (investigative); and C (change-oriented) or T (traditional).

Each one of the selections has its opposite way of taking in information, processing it, and making decisions or of organizing information, people, and objects.

Finally, enter the five letters of your highest scores on the line marked "**Your Choice.**" (On this classifier, this means your classified preferences based upon your personality selections, which means your level of comfort with your choices.) When you have found your five-letter choice, apply your selection to the description of job duties required in your occupation, career, or field of interest.

Note that you choose your personality preferences based solely upon what feels most comfortable to your health and creates the least anxiety, tension, and wear and tear on your body in the long run. Your goal is to be or become the right person in the right job.

1. You received an undergraduate degree online recently in computer game and animation design. This month you began an entry-level sales and marketing job with a major designer of video games. You would rather:
   - ❏ a. actively sell software by giving live presentations to audiences of vendors.
   - ❏ b. work alone at home online designing games that sell to a large audience and prefer to send your work by e-mail or disk to your employer, remaining invisible to the corporation.

2. You have time to practice your hobby. You choose to:
   - ❑ a. play martial arts video games for entertainment.
   - ❑ b. design programs to forecast future weather or stock market patterns.

3. You'd enjoy a job that requires you to:
   - ❑ a. select factual information from reports on tangible objects such as machines.
   - ❑ b. examine how radio talk show hosts affect peoples' attitudes or intangible ideas.

4. A Fortune 500 firm has two openings for a recent high-school graduate with no experience but good keyboarding ability. The job best fits his or her style is:
   - ❑ a. administrative assistant or trainee to a banking executive.
   - ❑ b. human resources personnel assistant or trainee to a corporate trainer.

5. When told to fire a co-worker for not fitting into the group, you:
   - ❑ a. terminate the person as you are directed to do.
   - ❑ b. advise the person to file a complaint for discrimination.

6. When asked to purchase a wide-screen monitor for your firm, you:
   - ❑ a. visit many stores looking for high quality at a lower price.
   - ❑ b. buy the first wide-screen monitor you find.

7. You paid a non-refundable deposit for a weeklong Alaskan cruise last year, but today you found out there's a weeklong convention in Paris that you'd rather attend during your short vacation. You are more comfortable:
   - ❑ a. sticking to your original plan and not losing your deposit.
   - ❑ b. losing your deposit but attending the convention in Paris.

8. To make yourself the center of attention at work, you'd rather:
   - ❑ a. fill in for your favorite radio talk show host.
   - ❑ b. write a weekly column for a local newspaper.

9. You'd take a job or open a business in order to have, above all:
   - ❑ a. job security, comfortable pay, but invisibility and familiar habit and habitat.
   - ❑ b. fame but a high probability of little income, rejection, and lots of innovation.

10. You'd rather take a job that uses your:
   - ❑ a. practical skills in repairing worldwide communications systems.
   - ❑ b. imagination to sell escape via virtual reality medical software for phobics.

11. You wish you had majored in:
    - ❑ a. business management.
    - ❑ b. professional writing.

12. If you were 18 again, the courses that would interest you most are:
    - ❑ a. math, science, engineering, banking, and technology.
    - ❑ b. writing, illustration, training, health, and human resources management.

13. You're asked to hand in an outline, proposal, and a report to your boss. You would:
    - ❑ a. plan your outline first, and then write your proposal from your outline.
    - ❑ b. write the report first and use what you've already written to design your outline, and select parts of your already-written report to include in your outline and proposal.

14. You're working on one project when you are interrupted by a phone call. You'd rather:
    - ❑ a. finish your work first and call the person back later.
    - ❑ b. drop what you're working on and gladly talk now.

15. At a party, meeting, or gathering you:
    - ❑ a. tell any stranger highlights from your life story to make small talk when asked from what region is your accent.
    - ❑ b. ask strangers, "Why is it important that you know?" when asked to reveal personal information such as the origin of your regional accent.

16. You want to keep your present but dull and routine job until:
    - ❑ a. you retire with pension, perks, and insurance at age 70, when you'll travel.
    - ❑ b. a job comes along soon where you can use your verve, vivacity, and gusto.

17. Once a week, your employer gives you an hour off for enrichment classes. The class you would take that's offered at work for free is:
    - ❑ a. home repair.
    - ❑ b. creative writing.

18. When asked to evaluate an employee, you'd first consider the worker's:
    - ❑ a. productivity in numbers and quantitative output.
    - ❑ b. words of warmth, inspiration, and job-related services.

19. The supervisor you would want as your boss is:
   - ❏ a. sarcastic Sidney, who wants to improve all employees' jobs by yelling at them.
   - ❏ b. gentle Jim, who's a compulsive liar, but very polite to your face.

20. When no one's watching you work at home, you:
   - ❏ a. start tomorrow's work when today's work is done, even if it's at night.
   - ❏ b. take off early to have fun, never thinking of work when not in the office.

21. Your work nearly always is:
   - ❏ a. on time and accurate due to painstaking patience and an eye for details.
   - ❏ b. somewhat late and in need of revision due to impatience and difficulty with details.

22. When training co-workers and executives, you're more at ease with:
   - ❏ a. giving a speech and training face to face.
   - ❏ b. distributing a training manual and teaching correspondence or online courses.

23. At work, you'd feel healthier and be happier as a:
   - ❏ a. trouble-shooter of accounting errors for a large institution.
   - ❏ b. tenured professor of anthropology.

24. You inherited an expensive, antique car that still runs, and now choose to:
   - ❏ a. keep it as an expensive, antique collectible.
   - ❏ b. sell it and buy a new model.

25. You would define time as:
   - ❏ a. an impersonal dimension of space.
   - ❏ b. a personal measure of the lifespan of any person or object.

26. The job you would take is:
   - ❏ a. designing back doors to computer software for government or business espionage.
   - ❏ b. investigating, as a journalist, government or business scandals.

27. You would rather:
   - ❏ a. follow directions to improve a system.
   - ❏ b. break rules to improve a system.

28. You're much better at:
   - ❏ a. time management.
   - ❏ b. adapting to changing schedules and swing shifts.

29. The job that is least stressful is:
    - ❑ a. receptionist for a busy dentist.
    - ❑ b. audio-to-text transcriber for an oral history library at a university.

30. You would find least stressful listening to a lecture that discusses:
    - ❑ a. common-sense, down-to-earth facts about cutting expenses.
    - ❑ b. the life spans of parallel universes separated from one another by membranes.

31. You'd rather work in the entertainment business as a:
    - ❑ a. marketing manager or intellectual property attorney.
    - ❑ b. scriptwriter, casting director, or animation designer.

32. People would say you value more:
    - ❑ a. what successful top management proposes.
    - ❑ b. what's in the employee suggestion box.

33. It's more important to you to be:
    - ❑ a. imitated at work for your financial success.
    - ❑ b. liked at work for your humanitarian volunteerism.

34. You want a job or business where you can:
    - ❑ a. thrive on order in one familiar place.
    - ❑ b. explore unknown adventures all over the world.

35. You prefer a job where you will:
    - ❑ a. complete projects where you see the results of your efforts.
    - ❑ b. get paid to play and have fun.

36. You would rather work in:
    - ❑ a. the telemarketing department talking to strangers.
    - ❑ b. operating a computer alone in your cubicle or home entering data.

37. You would rather spend the next 50 years:
    - ❑ a. as a repair technician by day and a video producer at night.
    - ❑ b. as a novelist by night and a psychologist by day.

38. You'd rather make choices and decisions based on:
    - ❑ a. your personal experiences.
    - ❑ b. clues and hunches found outside your personal experiences.

39. You'd like to meet people who are:
    - ❑ a. calm during crises.
    - ❑ b. figuratively able to walk a mile in your shoes.

40. If you could choose your mentor, the individual would:
    - ❑ a. welcome challenge and argument.
    - ❑ b. give up anything to have serenity and avoid conflict.

41. You would prefer to work with people who:
    - ❑ a. want you to keep every item in its place.
    - ❑ b. would wait as long as possible before telling you to put items away.

42. You're a human resources interviewer and would prefer that each job applicant:
    - ❑ a. arrive at the scheduled time.
    - ❑ b. come in without an appointment to chat.

43. You'd prefer to manage:
    - ❑ a. public relations.
    - ❑ b. systems.

44. You find the future:
    - ❑ a. scary.
    - ❑ b. exciting.

45. At school, you enjoyed courses that emphasized:
    - ❑ a. hands-on practice.
    - ❑ b. theories of future advances.

46. When machines break down in the office, you would prefer to:
    - ❑ a. keep priorities in perspective.
    - ❑ b. understand how error affects people.

47. In a new career, you'd rather:
    - ❑ a. solve technical or medical problems.
    - ❑ b. help people share meaning.

48. You are asked to write a simple how-to manual. You'd rather:
    - ❑ a. keep the original goal of clarity.
    - ❑ b. wait for more recent information to arrive to check consistency.

49. You would like to:
    - ❑ a. hurry decisions and finish the project quickly because the boss reduced the time allowed to make a good decision, which puts you under pressure and stress.
    - ❑ b. stop the staff from going with the first hasty decision because they've missed important details due to overlooked blind spots that might derail their careers early on.

50. In your job, you'd prefer to:
    - ❑ a. train co-workers.
    - ❑ b. monitor production.

51. You prefer to work with:
    - ❑ a. tangible appliances such as exercise equipment, computers, or cookers.
    - ❑ b. intangible ideas such as forecasting trends, cycles, or patterns.

52. You'd rather sell:
    - ❑ a. uniforms to healthcare personnel.
    - ❑ b. display advertising to restaurant owners.

53. Colleagues and family are most likely to describe you as a:
    - ❑ a. stern, competitive person who debated your way to success and won.
    - ❑ b. self-made, empathetic person who always puts the customer's needs first.

54. While training or presenting to co-workers, you'd rather:
    - ❑ a. convince your audience by logical analysis to clarify facts.
    - ❑ b. persuade the people by commitment to their values and identities.

55. When looking for a job you:
    - ❑ a. grab the first job you find that wants you to fulfill the company's goals.
    - ❑ b. switch jobs frequently until you find one that fits comfortably with your goals.

56. You want work that's:
    - ❑ a. reliable, well-organized, and orderly.
    - ❑ b. flexible, playful, and open-ended.

57. When many different people pick your brain all day it makes you feel:
    - ❑ a. eager to talk, bubbly, important, enlightened, and energized.
    - ❑ b. exhausted, crushed, drained, bored, and tense.

58. You'd prefer to use specialized software or books to:
    - ❑ a. invent a new board game.
    - ❑ b. teach in a computer camp.

59. The free lecture you would rather attend for an hour on a Monday afternoon is:
    - ❑ a. How to Improve Your Communication Skills.
    - ❑ b. How to Meet and Make Friends With Wealthy People.

60. When you read a book, you're more apt to see:
  - ❑ a. errors of clarity and typos.
  - ❑ b. how the book persuades readers to analyze values and relationships.

61. As a trainer, your students would evaluate you as an educator who is more interested in:
  - ❑ a. selling your ideas to your students than mentoring them.
  - ❑ b. the students' growth than in the subject that you're teaching.

62. You'd rather take a job where every working minute and keystroke of your day at the firm is:
  - ❑ a. planned, scheduled, and measured according to company rules.
  - ❑ b. free to create, rotate, and brainstorm as long as projects are in by the due date.

63. During weekends you:
  - ❑ a. make a list of what to buy at the supermarket and eat first.
  - ❑ b. buy food on impulse or by habit when you shop for groceries and go in hungry.

64. On your resume, you prefer to emphasize your:
  - ❑ a. interest in public speaking, training, selling, and giving presentations.
  - ❑ b. preference for writing, e-mail correspondence, e-mail interviews, and non-interest in face-to-face communication with your employers and co-workers.

65. You'd rather turn hard-to-read, how-to assembly or repair manuals into:
  - ❑ a. satirical reviews of their wordy short-comings on blogs (Web logs).
  - ❑ b. plain-language hands-on demonstration videos.

66. You'd rather repair:
  - ❑ a. machines and/or instruments.
  - ❑ b. relationships and/or attitudes.

67. You want to exit when:
  - ❑ a. co-workers cry in your presence.
  - ❑ b. you must terminate a co-worker for making too many errors.

68. You wish you could find the most persuasive words to:
  - ❑ a. confront discrimination in the workplace.
  - ❑ b. deny discrimination exists in your workplace.

69. What you need from your boss to do better work is:
    - ❑ a. a flow chart.
    - ❑ b. permission to diverge from your company's original plans.

70. At work you would rather have:
    - ❑ a. a daily record of every word said to you evaluating your work performance.
    - ❑ b. more self-determination.

71. You are willing to:
    - ❑ a. share spoken personal experiences with co-workers.
    - ❑ b. write a personal journal that only you will ever see.

72. On your resume, you'd prefer to list mainly:
    - ❑ a. skills related to a specific job description.
    - ❑ b. hobbies and groups that reflect your transferable creative talents.

73. As the new "employee of the month," the gifts you would like from your boss would be:
    - ❑ a. "G.I. Joe" type action figures for successfully beating the competition.
    - ❑ b. books on how loss of self during contests is viewed around the world.

74. You spend almost all your non-work hours:
    - ❑ a. feeling impatient about exploring alternatives.
    - ❑ b. collecting information and trivia that might come in handy some time.

Scoring

To score the classifier, add up the number of "a" answers and "b" answers, and enter the totals here:

Total A answers [   ]   Total B answers [   ]

Personality Opposites		
Grounded	↔	Verve
Rational	↔	Enthusiastic
Decisive	↔	Investigative
Loner	↔	Outgoing
Traditional	↔	Change-Driven

Transfer your totals of A answers and B answers to the appropriate section here.

Description	A Answers ☐	B Answers ☐
Part I: This score indicates whether you are more of a loner or more outgoing. Outgoing people usually enjoy being generalists who focus on breadth of knowledge, whereas loners usually feel happier and more comfortable at work being specialists, emphasizing depth of knowledge—but with versatility in fields related to or used in their specialty. A loner doesn't like to be constantly supervised or micromanaged. Loners, as introverts, feel stressed, drained, and wary or anxious by constant contact with people. Outgoing people are more at home with a wider variety of strangers and do not need to recharge before meeting strangers. Outgoing extroverts quickly find a connection and rapport with new clients, and they easily communicate with others. The goal of both loners and outgoing people need to be connection with others, but for different reasons and adjusted time segments.	Loner (L)	Outgoing (O)
Part II: This score determines whether you prefer to absorb real-world, present-day practical details through your vision, touch, smell, and hearing, or would rather take in theoretical, abstract information based on ideas or faith instead of present or historical proven facts. Down-to-earth, grounded people take in details by seeing, hearing, smelling, or touching tangible objects. Individuals with verve are vivacious, imaginative people full of gusto who prefer to take in information by focusing on the intangible ideas and abstract theories, vision, and beliefs of what could be possible with a extra exploration of what is real about reality. Those with verve prefer to state that our eyes or memory could deceive us regarding reality. Grounded, down-to-earth people may not have	Grounded (G)	Verve (V)

Description	A Answers ☐	B Answers ☐
as much verve, but they do have gumption and drive. They prefer to state concisely information that they can verify, see, touch, hear, or smell as reality. Down-to-earth individuals need to know that the facts aren't flawed.		

Part III:
 	
    This score shows whether your judgment is based on rational or enthusiastic processes. Enthusiastic people make decisions based on their gut feelings. Rational people decide according to a list of pros and cons. They weigh the negatives against the positives on their list and go with the greatest number when they add up the negatives and compare them against the positives before making a decision.
 	
    Rational people tell us to use our brain more and our reactions to events less before we act or make a decision. Rational fellows focus on critical thinking. Enthusiastic people emphasize speaking their minds, listening to healing sounds, and going with the flow of gut hunches, favorite dramas, cargo magic, mind-body-spirit research, body movements, connecting, and the sixth sense.
	Rational (R)	Enthusiastic (E)

Part IV:
 	
    This score reveals your tolerance for ambiguity and change. Decisive people are well organized, are methodical, and need to make quick decisions under the pressure of reduced time and stress. They may overlook vital information that they didn't take time to evaluate. By deciding so quickly, they could run into a blind spot that could derail their executive careers early-on.
 	
    So they have to learn to make decisions only after looking over the most valuable information needed to make a decision. Investigative people, on the other hand, like to wait until all the facts are in before making a decision. They enjoy investigating all the possibilities or alternatives before closing the book or signing the contracts. They don't want to overlook something important.
	Decisive (D)	Investigative (I)

Description	A Answers ☐	B Answers ☐

Part V:
    This score reveals how much you prefer to be driven by tradition or driven by a need for constant change. An example of a change-driven person would be one who needs to keep working on a new project frequently.
 	
    No sooner is your last project finished then you want to forget about it and go on to the next project. You'd do best in a job or your own business where you can work on different projects that gave you a chance to learn new information or skills.
 	
    If you're a traditional person rather than a change-driven individual, you'd be better off looking for work with a traditional company that offers you the security you need. It's more important to stay with a company and grow as long as you have the health insurance, promotions, benefits, vacations, pensions, and perks.
 	
    You wouldn't mind routine job tasks as much as the change-driven person. If you want to work for a forward-looking, change-driven firm that offers less security but more chance to explore, look for surprises with companies that are forward-looking or those that focus on new trends, such as think tanks. You won't be happy doing the same routine all day, such as teaching the same subject year after year or routine clerical tasks that never seem to change in scope.
	Traditional (T)	Change-Driven (C)

Circle the letter of your highest score in each part. Then write the letter in the corresponding blank spaces here to reveal your personality preference.

Your Choice:

Congratulations! You're an ___ ___ ___ ___ ___

? ? ? ? ? ? ? ?

Appendix F

Anne Hart's 100-Question Personality Feature Assessment

The purpose of this assessment is to determine whether a person is organized (neat, planning, methodical) or spontaneous (explorative, inquisitive, surprising, versatile); outgoing (extroverted) or a loner (introverted); change-oriented and visionary, or traditional and following successful historically famous people as role models.

The goal of this and other assessments is to show you your preferences on paper. That way, you can use your results to be only one of many guides you use to match yourself with an employer or corporation that is not totally opposite to your own personality styles. Personalities have many categories. This assessment is only one way of describing personality features. There are hundreds of ways of describing personality concepts. So, as a disclaimer, take it as entertainment to ponder if you're in a corporate setting, and don't take anything you see in any corporate-type personality test seriously, because you don't know which tests have been validated scientifically.

Many assessments are for team-building purposes. Others are for pointing a path where you can focus on improving any blind spots of overlooked information. The purpose of any test is self-insight. With the hundreds of tests floating around, trust only those that have been scientifically validated. (You'll find validated reviews of tests in your public or university library.) The rest, take for fun when not working too hard. What a variety of tests can do is motivate you to be creative and design your own tests customizing them individually for your specific job applications.

True False

☐   ☐ 1. Effortlessly, I tell nearly any stranger I meet about what hurts me. (*outgoing*)

☐   ☐ 2. At a party, I don't hesitate to tell anyone how I feel about the present. (*outgoing*)

☐   ☐ 3. I keep my bureau drawers, closets, files, or pantry neat and orderly. (*decisive*)

☐   ☐ 4. I don't feel other people are wasting my time when they talk to me. (*enthusiastic*)

☐   ☐ 5. I model my experiences after similar experiences of successful people.(*traditional*)

☐   ☐ 6. I prefer flexible time because I enjoy time I spend alone. (*investigative*)

☐   ☐ 7. When people treat me as a second-class citizen, I couldn't care less.(*enthusiastic*)

☐   ☐ 8. I work fine when my desk, office, or room is messy. (*investigative*)

☐   ☐ 9. Financially, I enjoy beating the competition. (*rational*)

☐   ☐ 10. When I finish one project, I want to forget it and start new tasks. (*change-oriented*)

☐   ☐ 11. At meetings, I'm energized by small talk with fascinating people.(*outgoing*)

☐   ☐ 12. When the boss says I did something wrong, I want to quit. (*enthusiastic*)

☐   ☐ 13. Every problem I solve is done systematically according to rules. (*traditional*)

☐   ☐ 14. I trust my doctor and dentist with my life.(*grounded*)

☐   ☐ 15. If a subject isn't hands-on useful, it wastes my time. (*grounded*)

☐   ☐ 16. I have never lied to anyone. (*traditional*)

☐   ☐ 17. I listen to the radio, movies, or TV so I won't have to talk to visitors. (*loner*)

☐   ☐ 18. I don't remember having felt stressed out with nervous exhaustion. (*decisive*)

☐   ☐ 19. I don't care that I make plenty of mistakes in my work. (*verve*)

☐   ☐ 20. If I can't be the leader, I won't join the group. (*rational*)

☐   ☐ 21. Life is boring when I can't apply or sell my original ideas. (*verve*)

True False

❏   ❏   22. I must frequently perform or express myself in front of an audience. (*outgoing*)

❏   ❏   23. The slightest trivia turns me loose in a rage of frustration. (*decisive*)

❏   ❏   24. Whatever I am thinking at the moment, I have to speak out loud. (*outgoing*)

❏   ❏   25. Every morning I go through the exact same motions of habit. (*grounded*)

❏   ❏   26. I can't beat people off with a stick; they cling to me for my advice. (*change-oriented*)

❏   ❏   27. "What are the rules?" is the first question I ask about any new job task. (*traditional*)

❏   ❏   28. I run home if at a party cameras or attention focuses on me in any way. (*loner*)

❏   ❏   29. Under stress, others go to pieces, but I calmly nurture them to health. (*investigative*)

❏   ❏   30. My house or desk is sloppy, and I don't care. (*verve*)

❏   ❏   31. In a long line at the post office or market, I feel angry or anxious. (*change-oriented*)

❏   ❏   32. I don't have any friends because they all betrayed my trust. (*loner*)

❏   ❏   33. I enjoy back-engineering or construction. (*rational*)

❏   ❏   34. The larger the audience the more I want to stand up and deliver. (*outgoing*)

❏   ❏   35. I can never sleep at night after talking a lot to people. (*loner*)

❏   ❏   36. If I can't keep my promise, I'll find someone else to take my place. (*decisive*)

❏   ❏   37. I'm so empathetic to people I'd walk a mile in their shoes. (*grounded*)

❏   ❏   38. When I read *Sense and Sensibility,* it resembles the story of my life. (*traditional*)

❏   ❏   39. One friend or spouse is enough company to nearly exhaust me. (*loner*)

❏   ❏   40. I'm always punctual for job interviews, travel, and parties. (*decisive*)

❏   ❏   41. I say "Fiddle Dee-Dee" and carry on in spite of war. (*investigative*)

True False

❏ ❏ 42. Laws, just as inventions, must be crushed before they can be improved. (*change-oriented*)

❏ ❏ 43. I manipulate people into doing whatever I want by sugar-coating tasks. (*investigative*)

❏ ❏ 44. I'm a "loose cannon" and can't connect at work because I'm theoretical. (*change-oriented*)

❏ ❏ 45. Surprise me anytime by visiting, as I get bored when I have to prepare. (*change-oriented*)

❏ ❏ 46. When an important test of my performance arrives, I run for the hills. (*enthusiastic*)

❏ ❏ 47. Anything I start I will turn in early, completed, and better than the rest. (*decisive*)

❏ ❏ 48. Confide in me because I'll go to jail before I'll reveal sources publicly. (*investigative*)

❏ ❏ 49. My nurturing flesh walks miles in your moccasins before judging you. (*grounded*)

❏ ❏ 50. I'm so practical that my "ship" is the tightest in the "shipping" industry. (*traditional*)

❏ ❏ 51. I feel healthiest alone in my room reading about other peoples' toys. (*loner*)

❏ ❏ 52. I'm so laid-back and mellow because life lightens up when I'm joyful. (*verve*)

❏ ❏ 53. I get too anxious when I plan ahead. So I need to surprise others. (*verve*)

❏ ❏ 54. I force people to give me what I need to keep me calm by playing sick. (*investigative*)

❏ ❏ 55. If I can't find trendier ways of solving problems, I hire those who will. (*investigative*)

❏ ❏ 56. If I'm alone too much, I get depressed until I call someone or visit. (*outgoing*)

❏ ❏ 57. I like loud music, racing, contests, and aggressive games or sports. (*outgoing*)

❏ ❏ 58. Don't surprise me with financial burdens or unexpected chores. (*change-oriented*)

❏ ❏ 59. Everyone leaves me their dirty plates to scrape, and I'm teed-off. (*loner*)

❏ ❏ 60. My antennae go up as a red flag when I sense I'm in danger. (*investigative*)

True False

❑ ❑ 61. I don't care about other people's personal values. (*verve*)

❑ ❑ 62. Heaven help you if you bust in on me when I'm thinking or sleeping. (*loner*)

❑ ❑ 63. I love to prioritize and multitask. (*decisive*)

❑ ❑ 64. Everybody makes mistakes just as I do, and I couldn't care less. (*enthusiastic*)

❑ ❑ 65. When I'm having fun doing work or play that I enjoy, time flies. (*verve*)

❑ ❑ 66. I won't study a subject or play a game if I can't be number one at it. (*rational*)

❑ ❑ 67. I'm investigative, theoretical, futuristic and creative but not practical. (*verve*)

❑ ❑ 68. Only my spouse/partner can make me mad enough to hit him or her. (*grounded*)

❑ ❑ 69. I avoid most situations where I could lose my balance or get hurt. (*grounded*)

❑ ❑ 70. I work only when inspired and then only in spurts right at deadline. (*change-oriented*)

❑ ❑ 71. With my long-suffering tolerance, I would make a great tutor. (*verve*)

❑ ❑ 72. I've never sassed anyone, used sarcasm, or talked back harshly. (*grounded*)

❑ ❑ 73. I walk in the middle of the road in my values and hindsight. (*grounded*)

❑ ❑ 74. Absolute silence is necessary before I can solve problems at work. (*loner*)

❑ ❑ 75. I manipulate rude people by enforcing consequences to their actions. (*rational*)

❑ ❑ 76. Each day is the first day of the rest of my joy and healing attitude. (*verve*)

❑ ❑ 77. I want people to argue with me so I can expose their flawed thinking. (*rational*)

❑ ❑ 78. I believe exploration and nosiness killed the cat. (*change-oriented*)

❑ ❑ 79. I don't think much. It's more important to express good vibes. (*enthusiastic*)

❑ ❑ 80. Someone is judging my flaws, culpability, and improbity. (*traditional*)

True False

☐ ☐ 81. If I can't answer everything correctly as number one, I've failed. (*rational*)

☐ ☐ 82. I'd rather retire than have someone criticize my work or chores. (*enthusiastic*)

☐ ☐ 83. I hate theories because every book written was done by humans. (*traditional*)

☐ ☐ 84. I don't have any friends other than my spouse. (*loner*)

☐ ☐ 85. In an emergency, I'm the first person to help the victim hands-on. (*traditional*)

☐ ☐ 86. I can't remember where I left my vital documents, keys, or glasses. (*rational*)

☐ ☐ 87. I must have the last word because I'm always right. (*change-oriented*)

☐ ☐ 88. I earn money from the prolific number of fresh ideas I generate. (*verve*)

☐ ☐ 89. Achievements have toughened me. (*grounded*)

☐ ☐ 90. I'm not sensitive to sentimental people. (*grounded*)

☐ ☐ 91. I focus on what's in front of my plate and not the future. (*traditional*)

☐ ☐ 92. I'm empathetic and sensitive to those who confide in me. (*enthusiastic*)

☐ ☐ 93. If my best friend said her mom shoplifts, I'd tell my mom. (*traditional*)

☐ ☐ 94. I can't keep a secret from the water cooler gossip. (*outgoing*)

☐ ☐ 95. I'd do anything to get attention. (*enthusiastic*)

☐ ☐ 96. I'm under-appreciated, underpaid, and invisible at work and at home. (*grounded*)

☐ ☐ 97. I want to fit in with a group and not be noticed in a crowd. (*traditional*)

☐ ☐ 98. I work with and discuss or think about only what I know. (*traditional*)

☐ ☐ 99. Winning is everything, even at the expense of the loser. (*rational*)

☐ ☐ 100. I love to take on other people's problems even if it makes me sick. (*enthusiastic*)

Scoring the Personality Feature Assessment

Calculate the total "True" answers and the total "False" answers.

If the sum of the "True" answers is a higher number than the sum of the "False" answers, then you know what personality style you have. The higher score number can be either "True" or "False." The question is not whether something is true or false, but what represents your own behavior and choice or preference in personality behavior. That's the way a psychological questionnaire works. It's the same on a test of emotional maturity as it is on a test of preferences and choices; it's an inventory. There are no wrong answers and no right answers. The score tells you what you prefer because that is what feels most comfortable for you and is your choice.

Category	Number of True Answers	Number of False Answers
Grounded		
Verve		
Rational		
Enthusiastic		
Traditional		
Change-Oriented		
Decisive		
Investigative		
Loner		
Outgoing		

The more similar answers you score on any one of the 10 categories, the more a particular concept dominates one or more of your personality features. The concept refers to the description of a personality trait.

Do you have more "True" answers or more "False" answers? Compare both sides. Use your score as a guidepost to explore further and check out other types of personality assessments in your library reviews of tests.

Remember that test answers can change depending upon your mood and attitude, so you should look at many tests before you decide what the "real" you is under differing circumstances.

? ? ? ? ? ? ? ?

Appendix G

Harcourt Assessment, Inc.'s
Simulated Tests

The following simulated tests from Harcourt Assessment, Inc. are copyrighted materials that are reproduced here by permission.

The *Bennett Mechanical Comprehension Test* (BMCT)

This depiction shows the type of illustrated test questions that are found on the BMCT.

DIRECTIONS

Fill in the requested information on your ANSWER SHEET.

Look at Sample X on this page. It shows two men carrying a weighted object on a plank, and it asks, "Which man carries more weight?" Because the object is closer to man "B" than to man "A," man "B" is shouldering more weight; so blacken the circle under "B" on your answer sheet. Now look at Sample Y and answer it yourself. Fill in the circle under the correct answer on your answer sheet.

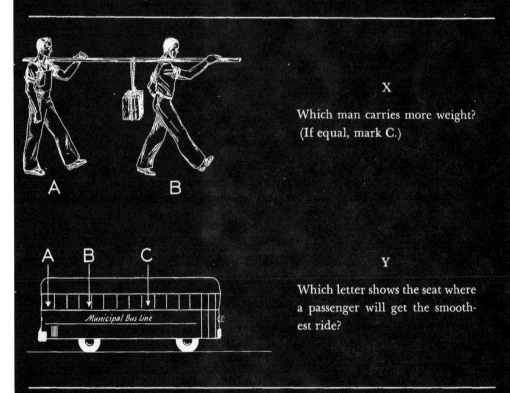

X

Which man carries more weight?
(If equal, mark C.)

Y

Which letter shows the seat where a passenger will get the smoothest ride?

On the following pages there are more pictures and questions. Read each question carefully, look at the picture, and fill in the circle under the best answer on the answer sheet. Make sure that your marks are heavy and black. Erase completely any answer you wish to change. Do not make any marks in this booklet.

DO NOT TURN OVER THE BOOKLET UNTIL YOU ARE TOLD TO DO SO.

The *Watson-Glaser Critical Thinking Appraisal*

This depiction shows the type of test questions that are found on the WGCTA. This simulation demonstrates the critical thinking required to come to a conclusion of the best answer. Notice how important it is to analyze the statement, before you can reach a proper answer.

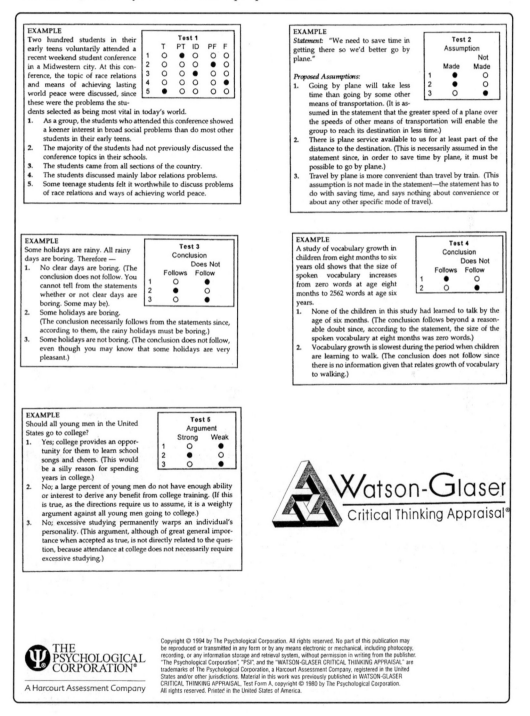

EXAMPLE

Two hundred students in their early teens voluntarily attended a recent weekend student conference in a Midwestern city. At this conference, the topic of race relations and means of achieving lasting world peace were discussed, since these were the problems the students selected as being most vital in today's world.

Test 1

	T	PT	ID	PF	F
1	O	●	O	O	O
2	O	O	O	●	O
3	O	O	●	O	O
4	O	O	O	O	●
5	●	O	O	O	O

1. As a group, the students who attended this conference showed a keener interest in broad social problems than do most other students in their early teens.
2. The majority of the students had not previously discussed the conference topics in their schools.
3. The students came from all sections of the country.
4. The students discussed mainly labor relations problems.
5. Some teenage students felt it worthwhile to discuss problems of race relations and ways of achieving world peace.

EXAMPLE

Statement: "We need to save time in getting there so we'd better go by plane."

Test 2

	Assumption	
	Made	Not Made
1	●	O
2	●	O
3	O	●

Proposed Assumptions:

1. Going by plane will take less time than going by some other means of transportation. (It is assumed in the statement that the greater speed of a plane over the speeds of other means of transportation will enable the group to reach its destination in less time.)
2. There is plane service available to us for at least part of the distance to the destination. (This is necessarily assumed in the statement since, in order to save time by plane, it must be possible to go by plane.)
3. Travel by plane is more convenient than travel by train. (This assumption is not made in the statement—the statement has to do with saving time, and says nothing about convenience or about any other specific mode of travel).

EXAMPLE

Some holidays are rainy. All rainy days are boring. Therefore —

Test 3

	Conclusion	
	Follows	Does Not Follow
1	O	●
2	●	O
3	O	●

1. No clear days are boring. (The conclusion does not follow. You cannot tell from the statements whether or not clear days are boring. Some may be).
2. Some holidays are boring. (The conclusion necessarily follows from the statements since, according to them, the rainy holidays must be boring.)
3. Some holidays are not boring. (The conclusion does not follow, even though you may know that some holidays are very pleasant.)

EXAMPLE

A study of vocabulary growth in children from eight months to six years old shows that the size of spoken vocabulary increases from zero words at age eight months to 2562 words at age six years.

Test 4

	Conclusion	
	Follows	Does Not Follow
1	●	O
2	O	●

1. None of the children in this study had learned to talk by the age of six months. (The conclusion follows beyond a reasonable doubt since, according to the statement, the size of the spoken vocabulary at eight months was zero words.)
2. Vocabulary growth is slowest during the period when children are learning to walk. (The conclusion does not follow since there is no information given that relates growth of vocabulary to walking.)

EXAMPLE

Should all young men in the United States go to college?

Test 5

	Argument	
	Strong	Weak
1	O	●
2	●	O
3	O	●

1. Yes; college provides an opportunity for them to learn school songs and cheers. (This would be a silly reason for spending years in college.)
2. No; a large percent of young men do not have enough ability or interest to derive any benefit from college training. (If this is true, as the directions require us to assume, it is a weighty argument against all young men going to college.)
3. No; excessive studying permanently warps an individual's personality. (This argument, although of great general importance when accepted as true, is not directly related to the question, because attendance at college does not necessarily require excessive studying.)

Watson-Glaser
Critical Thinking Appraisal®

The *Differential Aptitude Tests (DAT)*

This depiction shows various examples of the Differential Aptitude Tests. These multiple simulated examples demonstrate the types of questions found in tests of Verbal Reasoning, Spelling, Language Usage, Clerical Speed and Accuracy, Abstract Reasoning, Mechanical Reasoning and Space Relations.

VERBAL REASONING

DIRECTIONS

Find the space for Verbal Reasoning on the Answer Sheet.

Each sentence in this test has the first word and the last word left out. You are to pick out words that will fill the blanks so that the sentence will be true and sensible.

For each sentence you are to choose from among five pairs of words to fill the blanks. The first word of the pair you choose goes in the blank space at the beginning of the sentence; the second word of the pair goes in the blank at the end of the sentence. When you have picked the pair to fill in the blanks, mark the letter of that pair on the Answer Sheet, after the number of the sentence you are working on. Here are some examples:

Example X. . . . . . . is to water as eat is to . . . . . .

A continue —— drive
B foot —— enemy
C drink —— food
D girl —— industry
E drink —— enemy

Drink is to water as eat is to **food**. **Drink** is the first word of pair C and **food** is the second word of pair C, so the circle for C has been filled in on line X of your Answer Sheet.

Now look at the next example.

Example Y. . . . . . . is to night as breakfast is to . . . . . .

A supper —— corner
B gentle —— morning
C door —— corner
D flow —— enjoy
E supper —— morning

Supper is to night as breakfast is to **morning**. Pair E has both **supper** and **morning**; **supper** fits in the blank at the beginning of the sentence and **morning** fits in the blank at the end. On your Answer Sheet, the circle for E has been blackened on line Y to show that pair E is the right one.

Now do the next example yourself. Blacken the correct space on line Z of your Answer Sheet.

Example Z. . . . . . . is to one as second is to . . . . . .

A two —— middle
B first —— fire
C queen —— hill
D first —— two
E rain —— fire

First is to one as second is to **two**. **First** fits in the blank at the beginning of the sentence, and **two** belongs in the blank at the end. **First** and **two** make up pair D, so you should have filled in the circle for D on line Z of your Answer Sheet.

Fill in **only one** answer space for each sentence.

SPELLING

DIRECTIONS

Find the space for Spelling on the Answer Sheet.

This test is composed of a series of words. Some of them are correctly spelled; some are incorrectly spelled. You are to indicate whether each word is spelled right or wrong by blackening the proper circle on the Answer Sheet. If the spelling of the word is **right**, fill in the circle that has the R, for RIGHT. If it is spelled **wrong**, blacken the circle that has the W, for WRONG. Here are some examples:

     Examples

     W.   man

     X.   gurl

     Y.   catt

     Z.   dog

Lines W, X, Y, and Z have already been filled in correctly on your Answer Sheet.

There are 55 words in this test; you will have 6 minutes. Work as rapidly and as accurately as you can. If you are not sure of an answer, mark the choice that is your best guess.

LANGUAGE USAGE

DIRECTIONS

Find the space for Language Usage on the Answer Sheet.

This test consists of sentences, each divided into four parts, lettered A, B, C, and D. You are to consider each sentence as an example of formal, written English. In many of the sentences, one part has an error in punctuation, grammar, or capitalization. Decide which part, if any, is wrong. Then, on the Answer Sheet, fill in the circle that has the letter that matches the part of the sentence that has an error. Be sure the item number of the Answer Sheet is the same as that of the sentence on which you are working.

Some sentences have **no** error in any part. If there is no error in a sentence, fill in the circle for the letter N. Here are some examples:

Example X. I just / left / my friends / house.
           A   B   C   D

Example Y. Ain't we / going to / the office / next week?
           A   B   C   D

Example Z. I went / to a ball / game with / Jane.
           A   B   C   D

In Example X, **friends** should have an apostrophe; it must be **friend's** to be correct. Therefore, the circle for C has been filled in on line X of your Answer Sheet.

In Example Y, **ain't** is wrong, so the circle for A has been filled in on line Y of your Answer Sheet.

In Example Z there is no error, so the circle for N has been filled in on line Z of your Answer Sheet.

There is no more than one wrong part in any sentence. When you find a part with an error, blacken the circle with its letter on the Answer Sheet. Some of the sentences are entirely correct. If no part has an error, blacken the circle for N.

There are 30 sentences in this test; you will have 12 minutes. Work as rapidly and as accurately as you can. If you are not sure of an answer, mark the choice that is your best guess.

CLERICAL
SPEED AND ACCURACY

DIRECTIONS

Find the space on the Answer Sheet for **Part I** of Clerical Speed and Accuracy.

This is a test to see how quickly and accurately you can compare letter and number combinations. On the following pages are groups of these combinations; each test item contains five. These same combinations appear after the number for each test item on the Answer Sheet, but they are in a different order. You will notice that in each test item one of the five is **underlined.** You are to look at the **one** combination that is underlined, find the **same** one after that item number on the Answer Sheet, and fill in the circle under it.

The following examples have been marked correctly on your Answer Sheet. Note that the combination marked on the Answer Sheet must be exactly the same as the one that is underlined in the test item.

Examples

V. <u>AB</u> AC AD AE AF

W. aA aB BA Ba <u>Bb</u>

X. A7 7A B7 <u>7B</u> AB

Y. Aa Ba <u>bA</u> BA bB

Z. 3A 3B <u>33</u> B3 BB

If you finish the items in Part I before time is called, check your work. Do **not** turn to Part II until you are told to do so. Work as fast as you can.

You will have 3 minutes for each part of this test. Work as rapidly and as accurately as you can. If you are not sure of an answer, mark the choice that is your best guess.

ABSTRACT REASONING

DIRECTIONS

Find the space for Abstract Reasoning on the Answer Sheet.

In this test you will see rows of designs or figures like those below. Each row across the page is **one** problem. You are to mark your answers on the Answer Sheet.

Each row consists of four figures called Problem Figures and five called Answer Figures. The four Problem Figures make a series. You are to find out which one of the Answer Figures would be the next (or the fifth one) in the series of Problem Figures. Here are two examples:

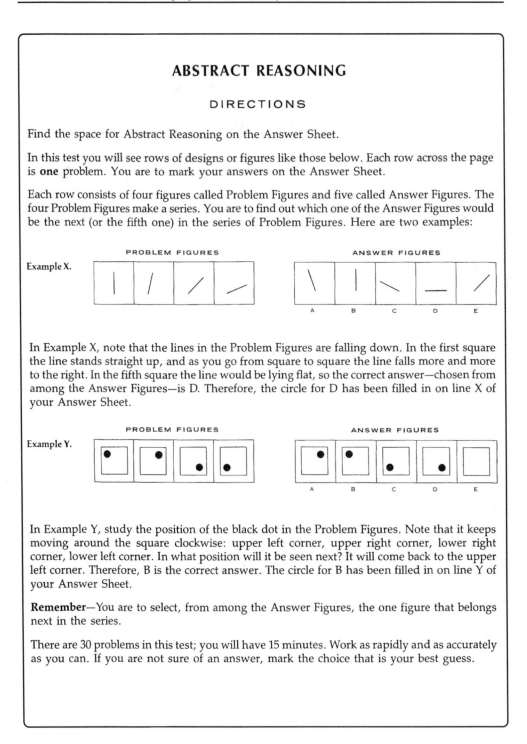

In Example X, note that the lines in the Problem Figures are falling down. In the first square the line stands straight up, and as you go from square to square the line falls more and more to the right. In the fifth square the line would be lying flat, so the correct answer—chosen from among the Answer Figures—is D. Therefore, the circle for D has been filled in on line X of your Answer Sheet.

In Example Y, study the position of the black dot in the Problem Figures. Note that it keeps moving around the square clockwise: upper left corner, upper right corner, lower right corner, lower left corner. In what position will it be seen next? It will come back to the upper left corner. Therefore, B is the correct answer. The circle for B has been filled in on line Y of your Answer Sheet.

Remember—You are to select, from among the Answer Figures, the one figure that belongs next in the series.

There are 30 problems in this test; you will have 15 minutes. Work as rapidly and as accurately as you can. If you are not sure of an answer, mark the choice that is your best guess.

MECHANICAL REASONING

DIRECTIONS

Find the space for Mechanical Reasoning on the Answer Sheet.

This test consists of a number of pictures and questions about those pictures. Look at the two examples below, to see just what to do.

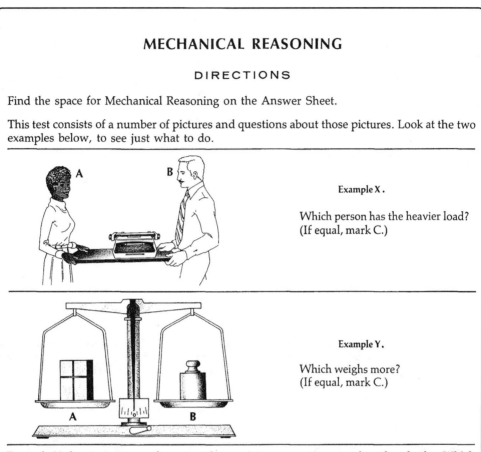

Example X.

Which person has the heavier load?
(If equal, mark C.)

Example Y.

Which weighs more?
(If equal, mark C.)

Example X shows a picture of two people carrying a typewriter on a board and asks, **Which person has the heavier load? (If equal, mark C.)** Person **B** has the heavier load because the weight is closer to him than to person **A.** Therefore, the circle for B has been filled in on line X of your Answer Sheet.

Now do the next one, Example Y, yourself. Mark the correct space on line Y of your Answer Sheet.

Example Y asks, **Which weighs more? (If equal, mark C.)** As the scale is perfectly balanced, **A** and **B** must weigh the same, so you should have filled in the circle for C on line Y of your Answer Sheet.

On the following pages there are more pictures and questions. Read each question carefully, look at the picture, and mark your answer on the Answer Sheet. Do not forget that there is a third choice for every question.

There are 45 questions in this test; you will have 20 minutes. Work as rapidly and as accurately as you can. If you are not sure of an answer, mark the choice that is your best guess.

SPACE RELATIONS

DIRECTIONS

Find the place for Space Relations on the Answer Sheet.

This test consists of patterns which can be folded into figures. To the right of each pattern there are four figures. You are to decide which **one** of these figures can be made from the pattern shown. The pattern always shows the **outside** of the figure. Here is an example:

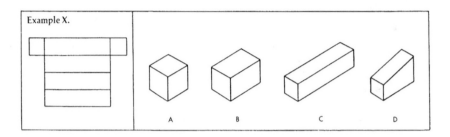

Example X.

In Example X, which one of the four figures—A, B, C, D—can be made from the pattern at the left? A and B certainly cannot be made; they are not the right shape. C is correct both in shape and size. You cannot make D from this pattern. Therefore, the circle for C has been filled in on line X of your Answer Sheet.

Remember: In this test there will always be a row of four figures following each pattern.

In every row there is only one correct figure.

Now look at Example Y on the next page.

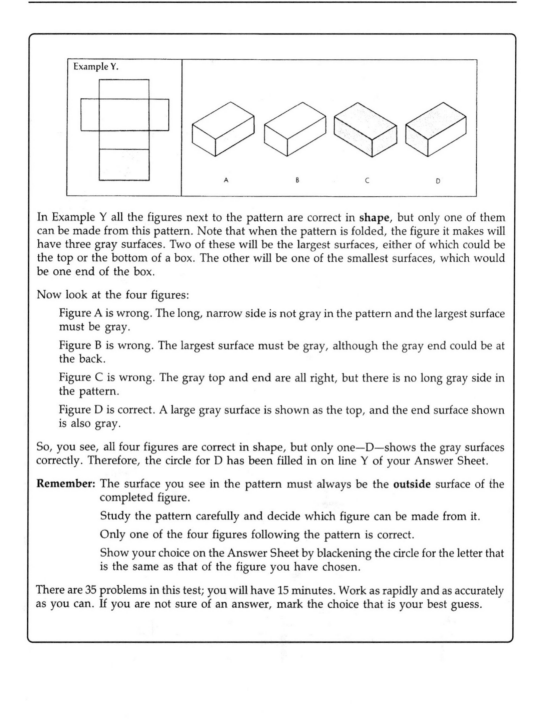

In Example Y all the figures next to the pattern are correct in **shape**, but only one of them can be made from this pattern. Note that when the pattern is folded, the figure it makes will have three gray surfaces. Two of these will be the largest surfaces, either of which could be the top or the bottom of a box. The other will be one of the smallest surfaces, which would be one end of the box.

Now look at the four figures:

> Figure A is wrong. The long, narrow side is not gray in the pattern and the largest surface must be gray.

> Figure B is wrong. The largest surface must be gray, although the gray end could be at the back.

> Figure C is wrong. The gray top and end are all right, but there is no long gray side in the pattern.

> Figure D is correct. A large gray surface is shown as the top, and the end surface shown is also gray.

So, you see, all four figures are correct in shape, but only one—D—shows the gray surfaces correctly. Therefore, the circle for D has been filled in on line Y of your Answer Sheet.

Remember: The surface you see in the pattern must always be the **outside** surface of the completed figure.

> Study the pattern carefully and decide which figure can be made from it.

> Only one of the four figures following the pattern is correct.

> Show your choice on the Answer Sheet by blackening the circle for the letter that is the same as that of the figure you have chosen.

There are 35 problems in this test; you will have 15 minutes. Work as rapidly and as accurately as you can. If you are not sure of an answer, mark the choice that is your best guess.

Raven's Progressive Matrices

Simulated items similar to those in the "Raven's Progressive Matrices—Standard Progressive Matrices" (copyright 1998, Harcourt Assessment, Inc.; reproduced with permission; all rights reserved.)

The Standard Progressive Matrices (SPM) consists of 60 items arranged in five sets (A, B, C, D, & E) of 12 items each. Each item contains a figure with a missing piece. Below the figure are either six (sets A & B) or eight (sets C through E) alternative pieces to complete the figure, only one of which is correct. Each set involves a different principle or "theme" for obtaining the missing piece, and within a set the items are roughly arranged in increasing order of difficulty. The raw score is typically converted to a percentile rank by using the appropriate norms. Raven's Progressive Matrices are widely used non-verbal intelligence tests. In each test item, one is asked to find the missing part required to complete a pattern. Each set of items gets progressively harder, requiring greater cognitive capacity to encode and analyze.

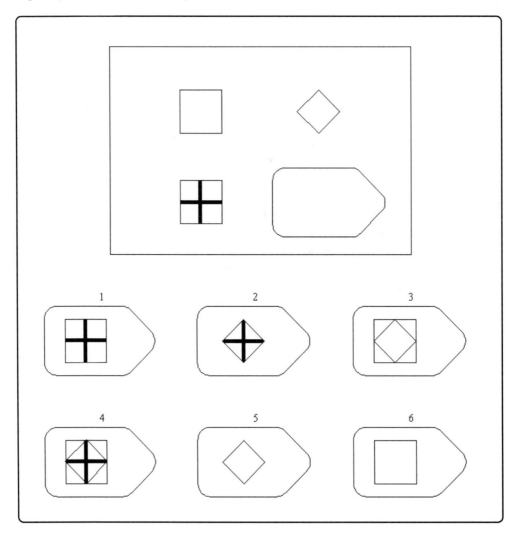

？ ？ ？ ？ ？ ？ ？ ？

Appendix H

Using Crossword Puzzles as Learning Tools

Anne Hart's Sample Bio-Inventory Test

This bio-inventory test tests knowledge of medical terminology for employees at any level who have to use, sell, read, or keyboard letters and other documents, or sell products containing medical or health-related terminology. It could be used to test anyone at any level from a medical transcriber, sales representative, or lab records clerk, to a student interested in interning with a DNA-testing company or nurses-in-training at all levels. Examples of who might take such bio-inventory tests could be traveling sales personnel selling software to healthcare-related corporations, insurance firms, hospitals, medical offices, government agencies, and DNA-testing companies.

A corporation might expect the test-takers to already have memorized the definitions if this bio-inventory tutorial emphasizes job skills over interest inventory, personality, or ability to look up word definitions as employees or job applicants encounter different job tasks.

As a variation on personality profiling using the tutorial method, it tests not only knowledge of medical/genetics terminology, but whether the test-taker has the personality-based interest in looking up the words in this un-timed test. (In an actual corporate setting, the test-taker would be provided with a glossary containing the words and definitions used on the test.) If the test-taker has the interest to look up the words in the glossary provided, the bio-inventory becomes a learning tool for genetics or medical terminology.

www.CrosswordWeaver.com

Clues

Across

4 High blood sugar disease

7 Neurosurgical procedure that can reduce many of the symptoms of Parkinson's disease

12 A mass of dilated veins in swollen tissue

15 Inability to make or use enough insulin disease

17 Cancer of the gland located near the male urethra

18 Wheezing allergy

21 Insert this straw-like instrument to draw off urine

24 _____ replacement

26 Type of anesthesia

29 _____ replacement

31 An incision (cut) into the colon (large intestine) to create an artificial opening

32 Valve Replacement

35 Tunnel

38 Surgery of the brain and nerves

40 _____ Fibrosis

41 Too much heat and sun cause_____

42 _____-heart surgery

43 _____ trials

45 _____ cancer

47 _____ surgery

50 Replacement of the pelvis and femur joint

51 Clouding of the eye lens

53 Relating to the heart

55 _____ cancer

56 Lying on your _____ facing up

59 Pain

61 Twisting of the intestine

62 _____ cancer

63 _____ Tunnel Syndrome

64 Out of sync

Down

1 _____ Palsy

2 Surgical removal of the uterus

3 _____ and sprains

5 Fibroids of the uterus

6 Metabolic "blood sugar" disease that may cause impaired vision

7 Device that keeps heart rhythm normal

8 Lateral Sclerosis

9 Roadway system inside the body (adjective)

10 _____ and adenoidectomy

11 _____ rehabilitation

13 Gallbladder removal

14 _____ aortic aneurysm

16 _____ replacement

18 Facial pimples and pustules

19 Surgery

20 for Surgery

22 _____ dysfunction, for which Viagra may be prescribed

23 Male sterilization

24 _____ replacement

25 _____ heart failure

27 _____ and Curettage

28 Total body hair loss due to autoimmune disease

30 A cut or gash

33 _____ Palsy

34 Joint pain

35 _____ Disease

36 _____ cancer

37 Lung surgery

39 _____ Barr

40 Cancer therapy

44 Type of laser correction for myopia and presbyopia

46 Acute infectious disease caused by the spore-forming bacterium *Bacillus anthracis*

48 Rehabilitation

49 _____ surgery

52 _____ therapy

53 Endarterectomy

54 Injections

57 Type of anesthesia

58 Obstructive Pulmonary Disease

60 Fibrillation

Numbered Solution

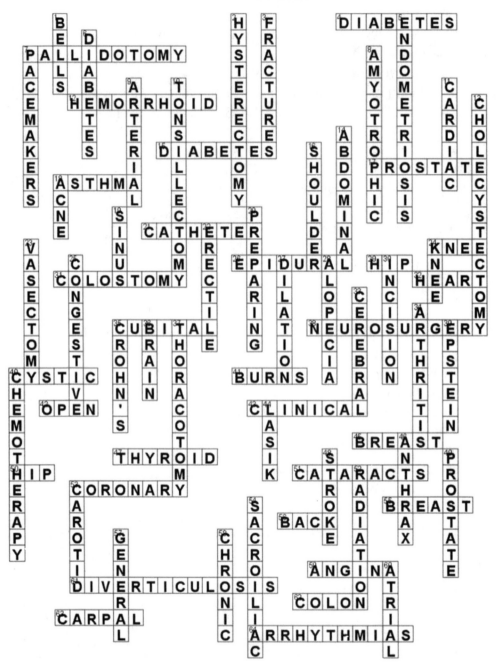

Creating Your Own Tests

The following puzzle is to help you, as a test-taker, to think verbally—to use the left hemisphere. The words don't matter, as this is not intended to teach anything specific.

Motivate yourself to create and design your own tests, customizing the questions to your specific job or business needs.

Sample Personality Profiling Puzzle

www.CrosswordWeaver.com

Clues

Across

1 A person's characteristics
3 _____ is always 20/20
8 Philosophy
12 Ability to direct
14 Choice
16 Examination
17 Vitality
19 Key
20 Purchase labor or parts from an outside vendor
22 Truthfulness
24 Abilities
29 Pondering
30 Alternatives
31 Sports groups
35 Perusal
37 Unity
40 Perceptive

42 TV or radio ads
44 Trainer
45 Type of activity that encourages teamwork
49 Vocation
52 Wrath
53 Seer
54 Structure
55 Quizzing
56 Working group
58 Trade
59 Abilities
61 Spoken
62 Executive ability
64 Relating to, occupying, or happening in space
65 Educational
66 Replace
67 CEO is an example

Down

2 Self-exploration
4 By numbers
5 Brain researcher
6 Logic
7 Pioneer of industrial psychology
9 Perceptive
10 For a short time
11 General understanding
13 Hobbies
15 Lucid
18 Creativity
21 Person who interprets quantitative tests to measure psychological variables
23 Managerial
25 Organization
26 Assets
27 Hidden hazards

28 Work out the details
32 Aptitude
33 See 23 Down
34 See as 64 Across
36 Connected with industries
37 Hobbies
38 General understanding
39 Spoken
41 Choices
43 Brains
46 Machine-like
47 Theoretical
48 According to time-honored practice
50 Dazzle
51 Process of evaluating processes to determine the best practice
57 Imperfect
60 Lennon partners with his IQ test
63 Perusal

Solution

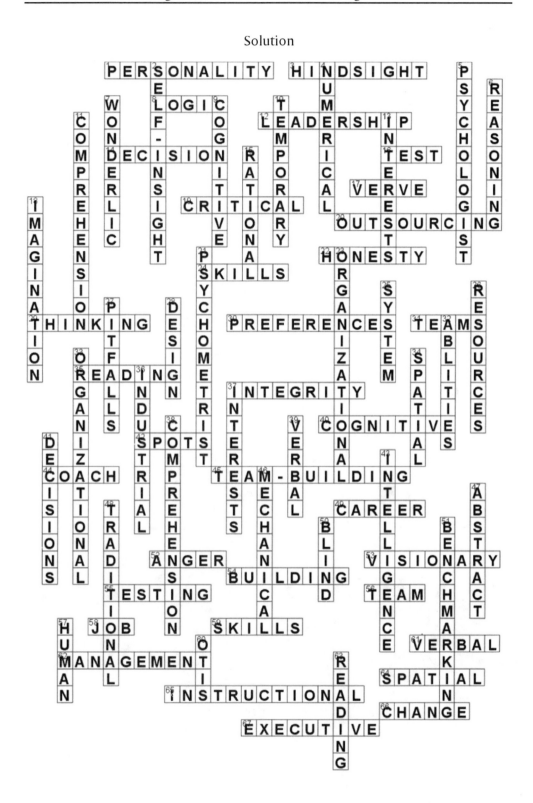

? ? ? ? ? ? ? ?

Appendix I

Essays as Values Assessments

Some industries require you to write an essay on your interests or values. Essays may be required if you apply to a school or for a teaching job, or for a job requiring writing or reporting information as part of the job, even writing memos or summaries of what you have experienced or found in your daily work if you are sent out to make a report. The following essay is that of a 16-year-old, female student at an Islamic high school in the United States. The essays gives the self-confident young woman a voice of resilience in planning her future, and the writing lets her show, in her own voice, her values.

"Why Is It All Normal?"

Life can't be described in one word. It can't be described in more than one word. There aren't enough words in any language. Knowledge isn't even a sea, or so I've heard. It's actually in reality, an expanding universe.

I learn so much, waking up and breathing everyday, almost routine, but I still learn so much. Life isn't so robotic, and redundant, unless you make it that way. You never learn from your mistakes, or the mistakes of others. That's just it right there, you can never put rules on how life runs itself, because there are rules for certain things, and for others it's just life. I realized so many new things about my life. I'll never get to a point of "saturation," "satisfaction," or "idleness."

I've felt so many new emotions and discovered new things about human nature. I write to my friend, e-mailing her the details of my accounts and anecdotes. Therefore I should have retained some accounts that I should relate to give a clear enough portrayal to prove my point.

I really try to share all that I learn, but sometimes it's difficult to communicate. I also should remember because I love to preserve a memory, which is why I photograph any occasion that I can. I would want to replay those memories again and again, to try to relive them. Sadly all the reminiscing can result in time consumption without result or gain.

It's not about self gain. Equate success to how much "memory" left behind, what you've done for others, nothing more. We are subject to mortal limitations. The evanescence lies in everything, don't deny it. I've been told to record my thoughts.

I've always seen written thoughts as "dangerous" but now, there are certain thoughts that are perilous, due to the boundaries of our complexities.

Every year I grow, and I think the middle teenage years are that of maturity like no other. Don't waste time, please. Ironically I feel that I could be wasting yours. Without any more of this vagueness, I will commence relating accounts you should find interest in.

You never thought that school could ever be fun, or life-altering. It was always so boring and routine. It was just something that you had to do, it was the only thing that you could do, so it was a time-consumer, that's all.

As a child, I didn't want to go to college. I didn't even think that I'd get to high school—not my grades; it just felt really far away (in time). School was always so far from what I wished it could be. I didn't like it that much.

My friends would come and go, and they still do to this day. Some leave because they didn't have enough money, some for their parents' jobs, some I'll never know. Others just grew apart from me.

I basically never actually had real friends. (Just one, but I only realized this about a year ago, or a year and a half ago.) It was a friendship that was said, not actually meant.

I tried. I really tried to make more friends or be friends when I said I was. I'm the kind who doesn't like to lie, especially to myself. I don't like illusions.

I don't like the fact that people like to live in dreams. And just because I have guts to say, "What's the point? We're going to die anyway." People say I'm too pessimistic. I like to think I'm more of a realist. I view things from a bigger outlook. I don't see life's events as a teenage drama. It's really simulated.

Teenagers are stupid, they make life the way they think it might be, and they dramatize everything. Matters are fine and teenagers make it seem like the world is falling out of orbit. Most are stable, and out of peer pressure (what a surprise, they create it), they lose control. It's completely pointless.

They force themselves to pretend to like the latest trends, or pretend to enjoy the new movies. I realized, I could do it, but like I said, I don't lie to myself. So I catch myself before I fall. I try to clear it up, and sometimes it doesn't work.

At parties, I dance with my friends, and I notice how others get attention, because they dance well, because they're creative, or they can bend in more than one way. Then I realize, wait, that's not a priority. I'm just supposed to have fun, and my dancing doesn't need to be like theirs', otherwise, it wouldn't be my style. Also, with trends, like the ripped jeans, I never bothered buying a pair. It's expensive and useless, clothes are supposed to cover.

Cell Phones

Do they have to have a camera, and mobile web, and those features that companies overcharge you for? Along with the 300-dollar phone, you get a plan that causes your bill to skyrocket. It's bad enough we have to pay for gas that's completely necessary, and completely draining us. Ask yourself, why in the world do you have AIM on your phone? You don't use it. Text messages I use, rather than calling, and talking on the phone, send a quick text. Did you buy a Razr too? If you did, it's a lucky guess.

Then again, people are experiencing a superficial prosperity, like the 1920s in America. How many credit cards do you have, how many "debt solution" companies are there?

Does it all make sense now? I hope it does. Read *The Great Gatsby* by F. Scott Fitzgerald. I did. Whoever knew I'd learn things from that? I read it late nights, with a bookmark that I sprayed with "Burberry" perfume so I wouldn't get bored. I did anyway.

I learned from it later. I like to experience, and then learn from mistakes. History repeats itself, and doesn't that mean that people never evolve? If the human race evolved, we really might be perfect beings by now, and that can't happen.

My junior year was a great experience, because the girls in my class were close to each other. There still is lack of trust, and close ties, and stuff like that. A friendship can't completely form except over time. Unfortunately, people breathe envy from their nostrils when they see us laughing and having fun together, so we pray we stay together.

I only have one real friend that has lasted for so long, she has my birthday, and she's two years younger. I don't always call her, but we're there for each other at special times, and we can call up each other like we've been together the day before. It's a beautiful thing.

She's been there since I could remember, but I have a really special friend that I met a few years ago. She's there good, and bad, and she never let go, and she's been through worse, that's even more beautiful.

We talk, and laugh, and we've become one person, she holds a piece of me now. I really don't know how I could live without her. She's like my biological sister, but I'm grateful she's not. Otherwise it wouldn't be the same.

I honestly have a story to tell for each day of junior year. It's amazing. We have something called "Hobo Friday." It's when the whole 11th grade class sat outside our homeroom and ate lunch together. We usually eat in the homeroom, but there's a class in there that day and we can't sit outside because of the bugs and dirt, and heat, and snow, and the lunch room is bootlegged.

My school is small, it's one building, and the gym, and the cafeteria is one place. The gym is small, on the top floor. The classrooms are not huge. The senior class was about 30 people, and the junior class was about 31, the other classes reached about 40, 50, about that much.

The parking lot is big, and the land area around is nice, but they can't create space (lebensraum). I learned this meant living space in German in my US History class. They are not allowed. My school also is private.

So we're lacking in so much more than I hoped for. Now I block it all out, it doesn't bother me that I don't have the chance like others do, and that I don't have the best people around me. Sadly I'm used to it.

A nail pricks me everyday, and I stopped crying. The mark is there, but I hide it. I appreciate what I have, and just live my life to the best ability that I can. That's what matters.

The bathrooms are on hiatus. They were painted by a few senior girls. The fountains are not drinkable. I warn people not to drink from them, and I think it's because my mom has inculcated the thought that I could get lead poisoning if I drank from the fountains.

The school has a really old heating system, and they can't fix it, it's too obsolete. I don't feel that my teachers really cared to teach me, except a few, like my history teacher, and my physics teacher. My math teachers, and other teachers too, but I don't need to mention them all, it's useless.

They were hard, and I regret that they were. I still believe I could have learned everything they wanted me to without having to work me like a pack mule. My Arabic teacher made fun of my accent.

I speak in the Syrian Dialect, and she doesn't. She wasn't encouraging, and I didn't like that. She made me want to never learn, or speak Arabic. I do speak, my friends like the way I do, it's different, and it's ludicrous when they try to imitate me. They embarrass Syrians, and I mean that as a joke.

We make fun of each other, and we always knew what to say. For example, making fun of vices and follies are our specialties. Once I was walking out of school. My mother always reminds me to concentrate and do one thing at a time, and to keep track of my surroundings.

I try to listen, but I failed myself. My brother has a G35 Coupe Infiniti 2004, and his friend has another sports car in the same color he does, midnight blue. They both have tinted windows, and it almost looks the same-to someone who's not paying attention. I wasn't paying attention, my brother called to me, and the cars were parked near each other. I was letting my instincts lead me, and like I said, it was feeling routine.

Usually the boys are around my brother's car, and this time they weren't, they were around his friend's car. I walked into his car.

I opened his door, and almost sat in. I got knocked into reality when my brother yelled out "What the hell are you doing?!"

Then I retreated and stopped thinking about my school events, and ran away with all the boys laughing at me, I sat in my brother's car after running around yelling "Oh my God! I'm so sorry!" They all laughed, and they made fun of me a few times after that. I let it fade away. My friend told me I was so zoned out, that she was calling me at that time, and I didn't hear a thing. High school is overrated.

I talk loud sometimes, and I love to have fun, and smile and I know that I have to make the best of time, even though I don't listen to that small voice inside. Sometimes I silence it, and that's not a good thing.

I know that I'm planning things, but I don't know the details of the event. For example, I was determined to go to my appointment to take off my braces, but I didn't know it would hurt, or that I'd end up staying at the orthodontist's for about 3 hours.

Also, I was determined one day to present my movie project for my English class, but I didn't know that I'd run around looking for things, and that I would have a hard time trying to find a projector and computer hook up for my VCD (no AV club, just a Computer Lab with all the AV equipment).

I also did know that my brother was responsible for us going to school and coming home, but I didn't know that for many days of his senior year, he'd make me run around last period looking for a ride home, or tell me to go home with other people. It gave a bad impression sometimes when I came up to people, "Hey, can I have a ride home?"

I had a lot of mixed emotions recently, similar to "I love it, but I hate it." I also realized that I don't go through half the mental and psychological problems a lot of kids go through in my age. It's mainly because I don't make my life a teenage drama, it's so pointless.

I'm probably a late bloomer relative to my contemporaries, but then again, they're actually early bloomers, but sadly it's not taboo to think or discuss what they do. They think about boys, and girls, and discuss gossip, and useless time consuming topics. Their minds wander into the "Twilight Zone" and places they shouldn't be.

They ask questions that they can't answer themselves. So they confuse and torture themselves relentlessly in their minds. They ask what if this

205

or that happened. Once during lunch, I walked away from girls in my class hoping they wouldn't realize I did, because they were discussing weird topics.

Instead they asked whether I was depressed. I'm not, I never was, and I don't plan on being that way. I spent most of my years finding myself, and keeping myself "grounded."

I don't remember being really happy in school, but rather more happy out of school. I'd laugh, but it hurt inside because it never felt like the second home it was supposed to be. I was more detached from it all. I was only attached because I had to be there. My parents couldn't think of an alternate solution. I usually put on an outside guise of "everything's peachy."

Depression

Do you know how evident and apparent it is? It's almost a plague. Zoloft, Ambien, and other sleep medications are being given out like Tylenol. "Hey you know your friend's father? Don't bother her, he has depression. And the other guy has schizophrenia." Why is it all *normal*?

Then again, like I always say, it's *all* a state of mind, love, composure, whatever you want. My friends said I sound like a hippie, as if they know the history of hippies. All they know is that hippies wear tie-dyed shirts, and have peace signs. It's all a state of mind, but I'm human. I'm never going to completely learn. I could keep writing, but I can't. I'd never finish.

It's the simple things in life, like the trips on holidays to the movies, bowling, shopping days, and parties. I don't see movies frequently.

Honestly, you always think you know what's best, what you want, what you need, but it's not true. You think you know that you need to do this or that, but you never know what's truly best for you. It's completely empty, a total void.

You think you're supposed to have fun, and go to parties (only girls), but that's materialistic, and selfish. Success is defined by you. I define it as being able to help others, and only achieve for others.

Now that high school is coming to an end, it seems so much better because I've come a long way from where I was—in a shell that I created. And now I have broken out. I've seen the surroundings, and sometimes I walk in the wrong direction but I go back, and I pick myself up and move on. Ignore me now, but never say I didn't warn you.

? ? ? ? ? ? ? ?

Bibliography

Dauber, Nick. *Barron's How to Prepare for the Certified Public Accountant Exam*. Hauppauge, N.Y.: Barron's, 1998.

Green, Sharon Weiner, and Ira Wolf. *Barron's How to Prepare for the GRE: 2006–2007*. Hauppauge, N.Y.: Barron's, 2005.

———. *Barron's How to Prepare for the SAT: 2006–2007*. Hauppauge, N.Y.: Barron's, 2006.

Hart, Anne. *Job Coach-Life Coach-Executive Coach-Letter & Resume-Writing Service: Step-by-Step Business Startup Manual Step-by-Step Business Startup Manual*. New York: ASJA Press, 2005.

Hoffman, Edward. *Ace the Corporate Personality Test*. New York: McGraw-Hill, 2000.

Kellogg, William O. *Barron's How to Prepare for the AP United States History Advanced Placement Examination*. Hauppauge, N.Y.: Barron's, 2004.

Lader, Curt. *Barron's How to Prepare for the AP US Government and Politics Advanced Placement Examination*. Hauppauge, N.Y.: Barron's, 2006.

Obrecht, Fred, and Boak Ferris. *Barron's How to Prepare for the California State University Writing Proficiency Exam*. Hauppauge, N.Y.: Barron's, 2004.

Parkinson, Mark. How to Master Personality Questionnaires. London: Kogan Page, 2000.

———. How to Master Psychometric tests, 3rd Edition. London: Kogan Page, 2004.

Seibel, H., K. Guyer, C. Mangum, and C. Conway. *Barron's How to Prepare for the New Medical College Admission Test MCAT.* Hauppauge, N.Y.: Barron's, 2006.

Tieger, Paul D. and Barbara Barron-Tieger. *Do What You Are: Discover the Perfect Career for You through the Secrets of Personality Type—Revised and Updated Edition Featuring E-careers for the 21st Century.* New York: Little Brown & Co., 2001.

Index

About the Authors

ANNE HART is a popular Sacramento, California, independent book author and behavioral science journalist, columnist, playwright and scriptwriter. She has authored 71-plus how-to books, numerous historical time-travel novels, and several plays and scripts. Anne is a member of the American Society of Journalists and Authors and Mensa, and holds a graduate degree in English/creative writing.

Anne specializes in writing about careers, ethnography subjects, current issues, women's interest, DNA, genealogy, and behavioral science topics. She also writes how-to articles for entrepreneurial magazines.

GEORGE SHELDON is a full-time writer, author, speaker, and photographer. He has published more than 1,000 articles and is the author of more than 25 books. His first Gettysburg book landed on the *Washington Post*'s Best-Selling List.

George co-founded the largest writer's organization in Central Pennsylvania. He has taught freelance writing to hundreds of participants of his writing courses and workshops and has mentored others to get their book published. He lives in Lancaster, Pennsylvania.